Humanitarianism

A Critical R
of Operation Life

by Larry Minear

in collaboration with

Tabyiegen Agnes Abuom
Eshetu Chole
Kosti Manibe
Abdul Mohammed
Jennefer Sebstad
Thomas G. Weiss

 The Red Sea Press, Inc.

15 Industry Court
Trenton, NJ 08638

 **Bread for the World**
Institute on Hunger and Development

802 Rhode Island Avenue NE
Washington, DC 20018

First edition 1991

The Red Sea Press, Inc.
15 Industry Court
Trenton, NJ 08638

Designed and typeset by Tracy Geoghegan

Cover photograph by Jeremy Hartley, UNICEF
Cover design by Tracy Geoghegan

ISBN 0-932415-65-2 cloth
ISBN 0-932415-66-0 paper

Co-published with:

Bread for the World
Institute on Hunger and Development
802 Rhode Island Avenue NE
Washington, DC 20018

Humanitarianism under Siege
A Critical Review
of Operation Lifeline Sudan

Preface

The idea for this study grew out of my personal experiences in the war zones of the southern Sudan where, during the past five years, the civilian population has suffered enormously. Yet politics has somehow managed to insulate itself from people's suffering and has frustrated repeated efforts to respond to massive human needs.

When after concerted pressure the two parties to the conflict agreed to allow Operation Lifeline Sudan to take place, those of us involved in humanitarian activities were elated. In subsequent months, some of us became seized with the idea of institutionalizing the principle of impartial humanitarian assistance in situations of armed conflict.

Our obsession grew as we realized that despite breakthroughs in other regions, war and conflicts, with all their ugly consequences, will continue in the Horn of Africa for the foreseeable future. Convinced that humanitarian principles should be the cords that bind us all, we began to see Lifeline as a starting point for legitimizing such principles in the region.

Many of us who started work as development economists during Africa's optimistic post-independence period have found development almost impossible in the Horn, given the stark reality of protracted civil conflicts. Most of us have ended up by default doing patch-up jobs as relief workers. Such work has exposed us to the magnitude of the conflicts and the nightmare of their devastation.

The historical circumstances that have given rise to the "just causes" of these wars are apparent: the legacy of colonial rule; economies geared to the extraction of wealth; boundaries shaped by the whims of outsiders; and political systems that have failed to accommodate diversity, facilitate popular participation, or sustain economic development. The inability of political leaders to fashion viable systems of governance has made for ongoing instability.

Yet the consequences of these just causes are tremendously costly. The catalog of human misery in the Horn of Africa makes chilling reading. Three to four million civilians have perished from war and famine since 1955. Over two million refugees have fled their homes across the frontiers of Somalia, Ethiopia, and the Sudan. Five and a half million people are currently threatened with death from war-induced starvation. These causes, however just, are destroying the very people whose interests they purport to serve.

The history of our region demonstrates that political leaders among both government and opposition forces alike too often consider the morality of their actions very narrowly. And while they may weigh their objectives against possible human losses and costs, they nevertheless engage in the most flagrant violations of accepted norms of conduct. Their excess zeal goes largely unchallenged.

Those of us committed to peace in the Horn recognize that its leaders will continue to fight to uphold their political principles. Yet we cannot accept the proposition that civilians should continue to pay the price. At a minimum, opposing sides should adhere to codes of conduct that recognize the right of third parties to protect civilian populations and provide them with humanitarian assistance. Lifeline has been a positive step in this direction.

Our study of Lifeline underscores the critical need for humanitarian norms to take firmer root in the region. These norms should blend universal humanitarian principles with traditional moral values that are the common heritage of people here. They should subject political acts to moral standards.

Ultimately, causes must be judged not only against the principles they espouse but also against the human price they exact. Our findings should encourage governments and opposition forces in the region to identify a core humanitarian ethic and to observe a universally accepted minimum code of conduct in war situations.

Today's heroes in the Horn of Africa are civilians enduring despite enormous suffering. Through this study we offer homage and respect to them and to those who have struggled tirelessly to maintain humanitarian access to them. It is my hope that this study and the continuing efforts of the Inter-Africa Group, a newly formed non-governmental organization promoting humanitarianism, peace, and development in the region, will help assure that the politics of the protagonists reflect a fuller acknowledgement of the consequences of war.

Abdul Mohammed
Nairobi, Kenya
June 1990

Foreword

In April 1989 the international community launched Operation Lifeline Sudan. The objective was to prevent a repetition of the experience of the previous year when some 250,000 persons are believed to have lost their lives in the Sudan due to civil war and famine.

Lifeline was made possible by an agreement negotiated by the United Nations (UN) with the government of the Sudan and the Sudan People's Liberation Movement and Army (SPLM/A) to allow humanitarian assistance to pass through certain "corridors of tranquility" to civilians on either side of the conflict.

Operation Lifeline Sudan is a story of a massive effort, led by the UN but building on and expanding the work of others, to provide aid to people under siege. The challenge was to reach more than two million people throughout the southern Sudan, an area about the size of Kenya, or of Spain and Portugal, or, in the United States, of Minnesota and the Dakotas.

Lifeline is also a story of the aid itself and of those providing it coming under siege as the warring parties threw up obstacles to reaching those in need. Difficulties notwithstanding, Lifeline succeeded in helping avoid widespread starvation and displacement in 1989. It has been extended for a second year.

The tactics used against the population in the grueling civil war were reminiscent of medieval military maneuvers. They included using relief as political and military weapons, attacking convoys seeking to supply beleaguered civilians, disrupting agricultural production and people's traditional means of coping with recurrent food shortages, and tightening the nooses around civilian populations in garrison towns and rural areas.

Yet the story of Lifeline is not a medieval morality play, chronicling the noble efforts of humanitarians to outwit the inhumanity of protagonists locked in mortal combat. The story is far more richly textured and ambiguous, multi-dimensional and convoluted. As written in mid-1990, the story does not have the happy ending of a morality play, though there are indeed lessons to be learned. Its telling engenders respect for the formidable obstacles faced and appreciation for the accomplishments of those involved.

Lifeline is a story of the warring parties themselves agreeing to the principle that civilians should not pay the price of the conflict in the form of hardship and starvation -- but then allowing other considerations to upstage humanitarian imperatives. It is also the story of aid agencies and personnel, humanitarian principles notwithstanding, becoming caught up in the conflict themselves.

Lifeline is not a single story but many stories. It is a story of desperate people receiving critically needed relief, of committed officials on both sides facilitating the aid effort, of dedicated national and expatriate personnel working tirelessly to pre-position foodstuffs before the mid-1989 rains rendered entire areas inaccessible. It is the story of east African governments speeding relief and of parliamentarians and publics around the world responding to urgent UN appeals.

Lifeline is also the story of concerted action coming years too late, of deliberate attempts to frustrate and obstruct efforts once agreed to, of an excess of humanitarian zeal and a dearth of aid professionalism.

Beyond the saga of high principle tested by day-to-day practice, Lifeline is also a story of personalities insisting that institutions live up to their missions. Lifeline reflected the passionate commitment and boundless energy of James P. Grant who, as Personal Representative of the UN Secretary-General, was perhaps its single most influential force. He made eight trips to the region in seven months to launch the initiative and keep it moving. Described in Churchillian terms by those who saw him in action, his ability to project the suffering of the Sudan's civilians onto the world stage has led admirers and critics alike to resonate to the description of Lifeline as "humanitarian theater."

Lifeline also reflected comparable passion and compassion among Sudanese in positions of authority. Grant's co-chairman at the Khartoum conference that launched Lifeline in early 1989 was Ahmed Abdul el Rahman, the Sudan's Minister of Social Affairs, an Arab from the north and a devout Muslim. Initially he shared the misgivings of fundamentalist colleagues about relief efforts. Yet he was so moved by the suffering of southerners witnessed on a visit to Abyei with UN officials in late 1988 that he took the lead in persuading the Prime Minister and a reluctant cabinet to allow Lifeline to proceed. He has told colleagues that he views his role in laying the groundwork for Lifeline with great personal and professional pride.

Commander Riak Macar, a senior SPLA commander in the western Upper Nile region who knew first-hand the hardship created by the war, took the lead in seeing to it that airstrips were quickly readied to speed the delivery of Lifeline food and medicines. He also took advantage of the Lifeline-related lull in the fighting to provide relief to members of opposing Arab militias who had laid down their arms and to resettle them in safer locales. The notion that assistance should be provided to innocent civilians irrespective of their location touched a chord in what the Sudanese consider their national character and brought out the best in people on both sides of the conflict.

Lifeline is also the story of people in positions of lesser authority, Sudanese and expatriates alike, accepting hardship and risking injury to see that relief reached those in need. It is the story of truck drivers and pilots venturing into unsafe territory and of railway workers interceding for the lives of UN officials with local militias. It is, at the end of the day, the story of Sudanese communities and individuals summoning up remarkable ingenuity and resourcefulness to cope with formidable adversity.

Lifeline's stories are divergent and contradictory. To some people, the initiative seemed transparently humanitarian, to others a Western and Christian maneuver to infiltrate an Arab and Muslim nation. Some credit Lifeline with embodying the ultimate in 21st century diplomacy; others see it as a profound embarrassment, a shotgun wedding on an international stage. In reality, Lifeline embodied elements of disinterested generosity and value-laden interventionism, of creative diplomacy and national humiliation.

The many stories associated with Lifeline do not lend themselves to being pieced together easily. Drawn from interviews with more than two hundred people in Africa, Europe, and North America (Appendix C), they form more a patchwork quilt than a whole cloth. While certain themes recur, no common patterns or easy generalizations by geography or politics, race or religion emerge. This narrative is a vehicle for letting those involved speak for themselves, however divergent their perspectives.

Lifeline is also a story of shifting realities. When launched in April 1989 its principles had the agreement of the elected government of Prime Minister Sadiq el Mahdi. They were reaffirmed by Lieutenant-General Omar Hasan Ahmad al-Bashir shortly after he assumed power in a military coup in June. However, aid activities thereafter fared less well, as did efforts to resolve the conflict beneath the suffering. In fact, some believe Sadiq's very cooperation with Lifeline contributed to his overthrow -- and to the tougher approach Bashir himself eventually took.

The military equation also shifted. Lifeline was launched at a time when each side for different reasons needed a reprieve. The cease-fires from which Lifeline benefited were extended a number of times, and with them the corridors of tranquility through which relief was allowed to pass to both sides. Yet both sides used the breathing spaces to consolidate their military power.

A year into Lifeline, the SPLA held more territory, and held it more firmly, than when Lifeline began. At the same time, the insurgents were on their way to becoming less of a military movement and more of a political and administrative authority. By late October, when the rains had passed, the war itself had rekindled.

There were also changes in the leadership of Lifeline. At the end of September, Grant handed over the reins to his successor Michael J. Priestley. The locus of coordination shifted from New York to Khartoum, a high-level diplomatic initiative evolving into a more routine relief operation. The SPLM/A, which had viewed Lifeline as heavily biased toward the Sudan government, had fresh grounds for unhappiness as more of the action seemed dictated by the Khartoum authorities. The Sudan government was already aggrieved with Lifeline at what it considered abuses by aid agencies and disproportionate benefits garnered by the insurgents.

Lifeline is also the story of the testing of international law and institutions by fire. Protagonists in struggles such as the Sudan's do not have unlimited freedom to wage their wars indiscriminately or to deny civilians access to impartial assistance. Yet here as elsewhere, agreed-upon international law gave way to political and military expediency.

The sovereignty exercised by the Sudan government to allow Lifeline to be mounted was soon invoked to assert greater control over relief activities. Aid institutions, many of them not accustomed to assisting in internal armed conflicts, failed to develop a common front for dealing with the authorities or to maintain an effective division of labor among themselves.

The situation is still too fluid to tell the Lifeline story definitively. When we submitted our proposal to do a case study of Operation Lifeline Sudan in November 1989, the war had flared afresh and Lifeline's future was itself in question. When our team met for the first time in Nairobi in March 1990, the launching of a second year of Lifeline had already been delayed for five months.

A day before our visit to the Kenya-Sudan border in late March, Toposa tribesmen armed with automatic weapons had overrun the area, killing thirteen persons and providing a fresh reminder of the vulnerability of civilians, aid operations, and personnel. In mid-April after we left Khartoum, an alleged coup attempt failed to topple the military government. The next day twenty eight persons were executed by firing squad at the order of a military tribunal, and in the coming months the government took additional reprisals against those suspected of disloyalty.

In early June, just prior to our final meetings in Nairobi, high-flying aircraft identified as Sudan air force planes bombed the SPLA-controlled town of Torit, hitting the hospital, a church, a school, and a market, killing seventeen and wounding over fifty, mostly women and children. The town, apparently devoid of military presence, was a center of relief and reconstruction work. One bomb hit a United Nations Children's Fund (UNICEF) poultry project, killing an attendant and many of the birds. The Torit incident threatened to delay implementation of the agreement to proceed with a second year of Lifeline.

Lifeline is also too current for its story be told with a clear sense of its enduring importance. If momentum is maintained and massive suffering averted a second year, the accomplishments of "Lifeline 1" will be enhanced, gaining still added luster if peace becomes a reality. On the other hand, if "Lifeline 2" becomes mired in continued political wrangling between protagonists or suffers from ebbing international support, Lifeline 1 may itself be tarnished.

Lifeline's value will also be enhanced if it becomes the basis for addressing the Sudan's languishing development agenda or offers pointers for resolving similar problems in other countries. Yet if Lifeline proves to have been only a spasm of worldwide concern which leaves national institutions in disarray and deepens international cynicism about large-scale relief programs, it will be judged more harshly as the years go by.

Even with the jury still out, the Lifeline story needs to be told. Many of those involved are still available to reflect on the interplay of humanitarian and political forces, on the personal and interpersonal chemistry that shaped the outcome. Individual agency evaluations to date have focused largely on technical matters, with little thought given by the UN system as a whole -- and even less by most governments and private relief groups -- to Lifeline's larger meaning. With the UN itself these days playing a more active role in regional problem solving and post-conflict reconstruction, its role in the Sudan is of particular interest.

Our first chapter provides historical context. Lifeline's success in meeting its own objectives, we find, must be viewed against the absence of effective international action in 1986-88, when the deaths of some 500,000 persons from famine and war are believed to have occurred. Chapter 2, which reviews Lifeline's work on a month-by-month basis, gives mixed reviews: positive in some aspects and negative in others, with some ambiguity throughout.

The next three chapters move beyond operational matters to the larger issues of politics, sovereignty, and peace. Chapter 3 looks at Lifeline's humanitarian activities in their political context and reviews their political motivations and repercussions. Chapter 4 examines the extent to which the exercise of sovereignty both accommodated and obstructed humanitarian action. Chapter 5 highlights the interaction between emergency aid and efforts to resolve the underlying conflict.

Ranging even more widely, Chapter 6 explores some of the implications of Lifeline for the future. It reflects the view that as the world enters a decade during which internal armed conflict promises to continue to take a heavy civilian toll, Lifeline's significance extends well beyond the Sudan. Its positive features, better understood, may become the basis for an improved system of international assistance and protection. Its negative aspects, if avoided, may strengthen future humanitarian efforts.

We wish to thank the agencies (Appendix D) that have supported our work. Cooperating fully with us, they have encouraged a critical and independent review of Lifeline. They believe, as do we, that a volume such as this is needed for the concerned international public on whose informed support continued humanitarian aid ultimately depends.

With that constituency in mind, we have kept footnotes to a minimum and have included illustrative material and a list of additional resources (Appendix E). There is also a glossary to help with the unavoidable acronyms. Quotations in our text, unless otherwise noted, are drawn from interviews conducted by the team between March and June 1990. Materials from other sources are footnoted. Quotations remain unattributed when information is sensitive and the sources vulnerable.

Beyond the general public, our volume is intended for government and UN officials and aid practitioners. Building on their interest in learning from the Lifeline experience, we are also preparing a separate document comprised of more detailed findings and recommendations. We are pleased that they have found our preliminary observations useful and plan to review our conclusions with them in due course.

We would also like to thank countless others who have provided assistance and encouragement. We are particularly grateful to those who have shared their reflections on Lifeline so generously and candidly. Without their help and the cooperation of a wider circle of people, we could not have carried out our research and published our findings within a six-month period.

Particular thanks are due to Church World Service of the National Council of Churches of Christ in the USA and to Lutheran World Relief for making my services available for this undertaking. We are also indebted to the Refugee Policy Group, which has acted as grantee for funds received and has provided counsel on our case study itself.

As team leader, I wish to express deep appreciation to my colleagues Agnes Abuom, Eshetu Chole, Kosti Manibe, Abdul Mohammed, Jennefer Sebstad, and Thomas Weiss (Appendix

F). The variety of our national backgrounds, academic training, and work experience has greatly enriched our work. Each of us has brought to our individual labors and corporate task not only hard-headed objectivity and seasoned judgment but also personal passion and humanitarian commitment.

While the data amassed, conclusions reached, and insights shared thus reflect a highly collaborative process, we have agreed that for purposes of consistency the finished product should be written by a single person. As that person, I accept full responsibility for this volume.

Larry Minear
Washington, DC
July 1990

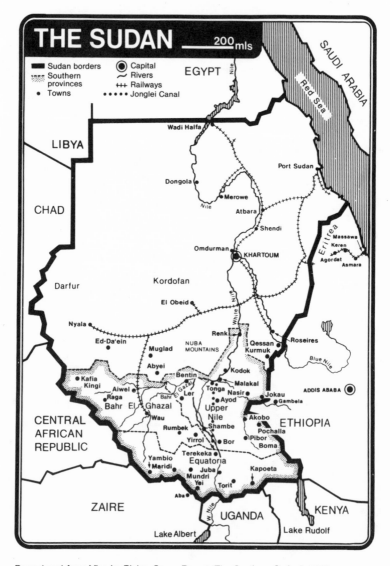

Reproduced from Minority Rights Group Report "The Southern Sudan", 1988

Chapter 1
The Background

One million people have died since fighting began in our country in
1983. Three million people are now displaced. Yet there is nothing in
your press about it. Are we not human beings?

The Rev. Ezekiel Kutjok, General Secretary
Sudan Council of Churches, March 1989

The famine and civil war that occasioned Lifeline have roots
deep in the Sudan's history. The more immediate stage was
set by food shortages, political unrest, and warfare during the
years 1983-88. The situation was complicated by serious
economic difficulties experienced by the Sudan and many other
African countries during the 1980s. A combination of historical, economic, political, military, and humanitarian factors thus
combined to form the backdrop for the launching of Lifeline in
early 1989.

The Sudan since Independence

The Sudan gained its independence from Great Britain in 1956.
Civil war has been a fact of life in two-thirds of the years of
its post-colonial existence. At the heart of the conflict has been
an amalgam of religious and racial, political and economic
tensions defying easy description.

The population of the north (see map, facing page) is largely
Muslim, with many identifying themselves as Arab. The
population of the south is largely black and practices
Christianity or traditional African religions. However, there are
Arabs trading and working in the south and blacks resident in
the north. There are Muslims among southern black Africans

and Christians among northern Arabs. In some parts of northern Bahr el Ghazal, Arabs and blacks are neighbors and have intermarried. In towns throughout the country, Arabs and Africans live as close neighbors and friends. Within the north and the south alike, there are widely diverse ethnic and tribal groupings with differing lifestyles and political allegiances. While regional religious and racial differences have become more sharply drawn in recent years, many believe they represent at most rationalizations for the conflict.

Recent years have also heightened the prominence of religious issues in the north itself. An increasingly assertive Muslim fundamentalism has made the imposition of religious law a crusade. This viewpoint has expressed itself in political terms through the National Islamic Front (NIF), a force to be reckoned with inside and outside most recent Sudanese regimes. The other major northern political parties, however, have Muslim bases too: the Umma party of the Ansar sect and the Democratic Union Party of the Khatmiya sect. The parties have also jockeyed for control of the various ministries in the shifting coalitions of a succession of governments.

The civil war has also been a time of heightened tribal tensions in the south. The leadership of the Southern People's Liberation Movement/Army (SPLM/A) is drawn largely from the Dinka, the south's largest tribe, which is concentrated in the Upper Nile and Bahr el Ghazal regions. The Dinka role in the insurgency has been exploited by the government to cultivate political differences along tribal lines. The government has used as proxies other tribes such as the Fertit, Nuer, Mundari, and Misiriya in its war against the SPLM/A. The war has injected a disturbing new element into tribal relations.

The conflict in the Sudan also has an important economic dimension. Major interest groups such as owners of large tracts of land, merchants, and traders compete for economic advantage and for influence in the government. While the

Sudan as a whole remains one of the poorest African countries, the distribution of the nation's wealth is heavily skewed along class and regional lines. Although the south probably has more arable land and more identified natural resources than the north, it has received less than its fair share over the years of government budget allocations, international aid, and commercial investment. Externally financed projects to develop the south's oil and water resources have triggered violence and memories of exploitation.

The military has also played a major role in recent history. For more than two-thirds of the years since independence, military regimes have been in control; civilian regimes, for less than a third of the time. General Jaafar el Nimeiri, who came to prominence in the country's first civil war, served on three separate occasions as the Sudan's president. He was replaced in 1985 by a transitional military council headed by Lieutenant-General Swar ad-Dahab, who was followed in 1986 by an elected Prime Minister, Sadiq el Mahdi, who was toppled by a coup in mid-1989 that brought to power Lieutenant-General Omar Hasan al-Bashir and the Revolutionary Command Council.

A major institution in Sudanese society, the armed forces have generally not been an active proponent of one political party or another. Southerners have served until recently in large numbers in the Sudanese army. Three of the ruling military officials in the current fifteen-person Revolutionary Command Council are blacks from the south. The SPLA itself was formed following a mutiny in July 1983 in the town of Bor by southerners within the national army's ranks.

As the shifting sequence of governments since independence suggests, a durable method of governing both north and south has proved elusive. Until very recently, Sudan enjoyed a tradition of democracy and free expression, enlivened by politically active trade unions and professional groups and by a media more free and assertive than in most other African nations. Yet at two major points in its post-independence history the Sudan's political and other differences have been played out on the battlefield.

The Sudan's first civil war, which lasted from 1955-1972, ended with Peace Accords signed in Addis Ababa, Ethiopia that promised the south more economic and political autonomy within a loosely federated Sudan. Civil war erupted again in 1983 when various provisions of the 1972 agreement were abrogated. A major grievance was the decision by then-President Nimeiri to impose *sharia*, a set of Muslim laws upon which are based criminal codes mandating heavy corporal punishments: for example, flogging for alcohol consumption and hand or foot amputation for theft.

The nature of the state -- whether it should be religious or secular, exclusive or inclusive -- has become the touchstone for the current civil war. Repeatedly disavowing any secessionist ambitions, the SPLM has affirmed its support for religious diversity within a single Sudan. The Sudanese government, with a Muslim majority and under pressure from Arab and Muslim fundamentalists elsewhere, has insisted on imposing *sharia*, at least in areas where Muslims are in a majority.[1]

The current conflict, devastating in its intensity and impact on civilian life in the north as well as the south, is putting great pressure on the traditions of tolerance and hospitality which Sudanese consider a central feature of their national identity. In a speech soon after taking power and reiterated frequently since then, General Bashir has spoken of the insurgents as brothers.

"Government forces and the SPLA speak the same language. Both suffer directly from the war, they are comrades, some are friends with each other and can therefore easily talk to and understand each other."[2]   The SPLA also speak in fraternal terms in describing their adversary.   Yet bitter strife threatens to undermine the ties that have traditionally bound together a diverse nation.   The Sudan's humanitarian emergency thus comes at a time of grave national crisis and is complicated by it.

The Immediate Past

For a decade following the Peace Accords that ended Sudan's civil war in 1972, the country enjoyed a period of relative tranquility.   From the outbreak of renewed hostilities in 1983 until Operation Lifeline Sudan was launched in early 1989, the country was engulfed in a widening vortex of violence, famine, suffering, and death.   Some of the events during this period are indicated in Appendix B.

Particularly in the northern and western parts of the country, 1984-85 were years of serious drought and famine.   It was also a time when more than half a million persons from neighboring Tigray and Eritrea sought refuge in the Sudan, taking advantage of traditional Sudanese hospitality but taxing the government's capacity to respond.   More than fifty non-governmental organizations (NGOs) lent a helping hand to the displaced, both Sudanese and Ethiopian.   With the immediate famine situation largely controlled by 1986, the scene shifted to the south.   Spared the worst of the drought in 1984-85, it was particularly hard hit during the years 1986-88.

Food shortages due to inadequate rainfall would have been more manageable without the civil war.   Internal armed conflict, however, flared afresh in 1983, complicating the picture enormously.   Both major protagonists adopted military policies that directly and indirectly created famine and other hardships.   These policies disrupted normal agricultural and economic life, forcing people to migrate away from roads and into towns or out of the south altogether. As part of its military strategy to contain the spread of the rebellion, the government equipped tribal militias with sophisticated weapons that were then turned against civilian populations suspected of loyalty to the SPLM/A. The insurgents tightened the noose on government-held garrison towns to apply pressure on Khartoum authorities.

The scale of suffering during the mid-eighties was staggering. UN figures put the number of southerners displaced during 1986-88 at some three million, or half the estimated population of the south. Given the extended family system, virtually every family unit was affected. Deaths during the years 1986-88 are placed between 400,000 and 500,000 persons. The UN estimates deaths related to war and famine in 1988 alone at 250,000. Half of these were children but only 6,000 were soldiers. Experts view the famine itself as one of the most withering in modern times in terms of severity, scale, and duration.

Throughout the five years of rekindled conflict and worsening food shortages that preceded Lifeline, various attempts were made to deal with the needs of civilians. Early on, the lead was taken by indigenous Sudanese NGOs, sometimes in concert with UN officials. With most expatriate NGOs and other aid agencies preoccupied with the drought in the north, little international monitoring of developments in the south was taking place otherwise. Governments, many of them with ties to Khartoum, were not inclined to involve themselves in the civil war, even from a humanitarian viewpoint, and preferred to give the newly elected government of Prime Minister Sadiq el Mahdi a breathing spell.

The complex political and military situation required aid officials to deal with both protagonists, neither of whom welcomed relief assistance to the other. Many government-held towns were surrounded by countryside controlled by the insurgents. Rural areas were themselves subject to attack by government troops. In some locales, areas controlled by one warring party or the other, or contested by each, existed side-by-side. The war had no formal or fixed battle lines, consisting at any given time of pockets of active fighting. The need for the safe passage of relief aid was thus critical.

In early 1986, the Sudan Council of Churches (SCC), an ecumenical grouping of the country's Protestant and Catholic churches, and Sudanaid, the relief and development arm of the Sudan Bishops' Conference, alerted international aid agencies to food shortages in the south and to the interference of the war with the region's recovery from the drought. They estimated that thirty percent of the population had already been displaced. With their prodding and with encouragement from other NGOs such as Oxfam-UK and from UNICEF and donor governments, the Sudan government set up a committee which, ever since, has monitored the situation.

In 1986, the same two groups with the help of local church leaders from the Upper Nile area negotiated a safe passage agreement for relief supplies into a region that had been without food shipments for two years. Local government authorities and SPLA commanders allowed a barge convoy to supply people on both sides of the conflict. UNICEF provided some of the supplies.

At the urging of local church leaders and tribal chiefs and after negotiations with the authorities, the SCC in 1987 mounted a vaccination program for over 50,000 head of cattle. This was a priority for people in both government and SPLA-controlled rural areas, for whom livestock represented an important nutritional and economic asset. While the benefits of initiatives such as these were real, they were time-consuming to negotiate and implement and their scale was limited.

NGO efforts from 1986 on to provide food to the Equatoria region from neighboring Kenya also encountered serious difficulties. The insurgents were reluctant to let food pass through territory they held to the government-controlled town of Juba, while the government gave no assurances that its troops would not attack food bound for insurgent-held areas. Despite the uncertainties and with some help from the European Community (EC), private agencies set up a coordinated relief effort in Juba called CART (Combined Agencies Relief Team), which has continued to distribute supplies after they reach the city. Oxfam-UK also embarked on a major cattle vaccination program in the Equatoria region.

A severely malnourished Sudanese child with mother and sibling.
UNICEF/Edith Simmons

In 1986 World Vision International, in collaboration with the Sudan Council of Churches and Sudanaid, undertook a major initiative. In response to an anguished appeal from the Bishop of Wau, a government-held town besieged by the SPLA, the groups came to the aid of beleaguered civilians with over 2,000 tons of food and other items transported from the north. The success of the operation encouraged NGOs to establish a system in western Equatoria that would allow them to supply Wau with food flown in from nearby Zaire.

The first major UN initiative in the south came with Operation Rainbow in 1986. Supported by eleven donor governments, the effort to supply civilians on both sides was spearheaded by Winston Prattley, Sudan Representative of the UN Secretary-General, and managed by Stefan da Mistura of the World Food Programme (WFP). It encountered problems from both sides, neither of which acknowledged the scale of the need nor wanted relief to go to the other. The SPLA threatened to shoot down relief planes bound for the government-held towns of Juba, Wau, and Malakal that it had not cleared. The government offered no guarantees of safety either. Its expulsion of Prattley, declared persona non grata in late October for his association with efforts to find a way to assist on both sides, sent a chilling message.

In 1987, UNICEF, WFP, and NGOs such as the French Médecins sans Frontières-France and the Irish Concern sent a team to review the critical situation in El Meiram, a transit point on the route to Khartoum for people fleeing the violence in the Bahr el Ghazal area. UNICEF's representative in Khartoum, Cole Dodge, seeking to regain momentum lost following the setback to Operation Rainbow, pressed the government to allow relief to be provided to civilians in such straits. He obtained the Prime Minister's agreement to airlift medicine to both sides, with the SPLA concurring reluctantly. International pressure grew as human rights abuses became more widely known. The publication in July of a work by two Sudanese university lecturers depicted the resurgence of slavery as a result of militia activities and the massacre of Dinkas in Wau by the army and tribal militias.

Dodge and his idea of a major humanitarian assistance effort, however, antagonized Muslim fundamentalists in the government. Under pressure from Khartoum, which requested his reassignment in late 1988, UNICEF transferred Dodge out of the country early the next year. In late 1987, the Sudan authorities had also expelled four private religious groups

---

Survey Mission to Aweil
November 30-December 1, 1988

We were given a detailed description of the tragedy which had its peak between June and September 1988 when nearly 8,000 people died in the town [of Aweil] alone due to lack of food. No information is available about what happened outside the town during this period. The approximately 30,000 survivors living in Aweil town bear the marks of this disaster. They have all come through a traumatic experience and there is a deep longing for peace....

At present approximately one quarter of all children must be considered severely malnourished and one quarter moderately malnourished [based on a survey] of 160 children selected at random. We have concluded that the majority of all children below five years are malnourished, a very alarming number, considering they are the survivors of a famine....

The death rate of children below five years was 25.88 per 10,000 children per day calculated over a period of 180 days between June and November, 1988. This very high infant mortality must also be attributed to a measles epidemic during the same period. No vaccination programs were carried out in Aweil in the past. This rate seems to have come down now. The weak have vanished and around the town one can see the signs of burials in improvised graveyards.

United Nations Development Programme
Khartoum, Sudan

associated with efforts to assist in the south: the Lutheran World Federation (LWF), World Vision International, Association of Christian Resource Organizations Serving Sudan (ACROSS), and the Swedish Free Mission.

For most of 1988, efforts by the International Committee of the Red Cross (ICRC) to get both parties to agree to its delivery of relief supplies were also frustrated. Faithful to its charter which requires transparent dealings with both sides, the ICRC labored from March, when it first proposed the idea, until December, when its first flights took place, before satisfactory arrangements were worked out. First one side and then the other objected. (See box, p. 135)

With the suffering of the civilian population worsening and agreement by both sides on relief activities proving elusive, more attention was directed by private aid groups to helping people on one side only. During 1988, a number of cross-border operations were mounted into the south from Kenya and Uganda. Those bound for government-held areas were undertaken with the knowledge and blessing of the Sudan government; those headed for SPLA-controlled areas went forward without its approval.

Several religious groups took the lead in supplying the government-held town of Juba, under siege since 1986. (See box, p. 72) Recently expelled by the Sudan government, LWF mounted an airlift from Nairobi which, with food donated by the EC and funds provided by various governments, became the major external food source for Juba's civilian population for over a year. Catholic Relief Services operated an airlift from nearby Uganda using commodities provided by WFP. Church World Service arranged overland transport to Juba from Kenya for food commodities provided by the US government until the effort encountered security problems and was suspended.

Meanwhile, other groups were assisting people in SPLA-controlled areas. In late 1987 Norwegian People's Aid (NPA) began road and air transport of medical and other supplies and personnel from Nairobi. World Vision International, in partnership with NPA, provided US government food to people in SPLA-controlled areas as well as, on its own, to the government-controlled town of Wau. These and other groups such as MSF-Holland had already delivered substantial quantities of relief supplies to the south by the time Lifeline began.

Such efforts were highly vulnerable. In an escalating spiral of attacks during 1986-88, the SPLA targeted vehicles, some of which were seeking to provide humanitarian aid, on the grounds that they also contained military items. In 1986, the SPLA downed a UNICEF plane in March, attacked an overland convoy in June, shot down a civilian airplane in August, and attacked a barge convoy in December. In 1987, the SPLA attacked a convoy of food trucks in September and barges in March, relief aircraft in August, and a commercial passenger plane in May. In 1988 the SPLA attacked truck convoys in February, June, and September, barges in February, and relief flights in February, March, and September, bringing down another civilian aircraft in November. The toll in lost lives and supplies was substantial, as was the disruption of relief activities.[3]

While the Sudan government was perhaps less frontal in its assault on relief efforts, it, too, managed to frustrate attempts to supply civilians in the south. It maintained that relief could only be provided in the areas it controlled, where it supervised relief activities closely, and withheld permission for agencies to operate elsewhere. For their part, the insurgents held that relief should be provided to people on both sides but that if civilians in SPLA areas were not to benefit, neither would civilians elsewhere.

Growing concern about war and famine in the south was also affected by a natural disaster that struck Khartoum in August 1988. Heavy rains and subsequent flooding created additional misery among the estimated 1.5 million displaced persons who had fled the violence in the south to shanty towns around Khartoum. Only with the floods, reports a UN official, "were we able to make references to those people who had arrived in Khartoum as displaced from the south" and to arrange for them and for those who remained behind. The floods also generated media coverage, which had been sparse during the earlier years of war and famine, and attracted some aid.

Throughout the years that preceded Lifeline, then, relief efforts encountered serious difficulties. First, political authorities on both sides were preoccupied with fighting the war rather than with relieving the suffering it was creating. Each side was willing to go to great lengths to prevent supplies, including humanitarian assistance, from reaching its adversary. Apprehensive about such relief activities as were nonetheless mounted, they insisted on being kept fully in the picture and on playing a major role themselves.

Second, political and military constraints were complicated by formidable logistical problems. People who were short of food and uprooted by the war were spread across an enormous territory. Many of them were not reachable during the rainy season by road and other means of transport were not readily available. At the same time, even displaced civilians near Khartoum who were more easily accessible received little aid.

Even if political and logistical difficulties had been overcome, the scale of the emergency during the latter part of 1988 and in early 1989 was outrunning the ability of piecemeal efforts to cope with it. The government itself was becoming increasingly alarmed. In June 1988 it requested UN Secretary-General Javier Pérez de Cuéllar to appeal for international assistance to prevent starvation in the south and among the displaced around Khartoum. The Secretary-General sent fact-finding missions to the Sudan in July and September but their work was interrupted by the August floods.

In October the UN General Assembly, following a review of the Secretary-General's recommendations, requested him to mobilize and coordinate a major relief and reconstruction effort. He then declared an emergency, issued an appeal for funds, and instructed the UN staff in Khartoum to step up existing relief activities and planning. In November UN officials reported on the humanitarian needs in the Sudan emergency and in December the General Assembly called for a conference on the crisis.

The stage was thus set for Operation Lifeline Sudan. Its challenge would be to succeed where a host of previous efforts had proved too little and too late. Whatever it accomplished -- the subject of the following chapter -- would be tempered by the realization that the international community bestirred itself into action only after three years during which half a million people had died. While success would have to be built on failure, there was at least enough recent experience to provide sound guidance.

Launching Lifeline

The Conference on Relief Operations was held March 8-9, 1989 in Khartoum. Hosted by the Sudan government and the UN, it drew together Sudan government officials and the aid staffs of Western governments, UN agencies, and NGOs. Its purpose was to launch a concerted effort to avoid a repetition of the disastrous experience of the previous year. "Aid agencies work against time and Sudan's conflicts," ran the headline of a March 13 report in the British newspaper *The Independent*.

Prime Minister Sadiq el Mahdi (in *kaffiyeh*) opens the Khartoum Conference on Lifeline. Also pictured are Sudanese government and UN officials.
UNICEF/Jeremy Hartley

The meeting took place in an atmosphere of widespread skepticism. The challenge confronting the international community was daunting. In the midst of a civil war in which the protagonists for years had obstructed relief efforts and in which territory was still changing hands, substantial amounts of food needed to reach people quickly before rains rendered vast areas totally inaccessible. The task was so formidable that some opposed calling a conference or mounting a major operation at all.

Such misgivings appeared well-founded. Most of the twenty donor countries represented at the conference, which had been delayed from February, sent Khartoum-based staff rather than officials from their national capitals. The meeting was delayed further to allow Prime Minister Sadiq el Mahdi, who would open it, to return from a brief political mission to Libya. The insurgents, who were not present, denounced holding the session in their opponents' capital as "illegal and a deep conspiracy." They had to be enlisted later.

The plan of action for the relief effort had been pieced together at the last minute. Based on an assessment of emergency needs for food and other supplies during the period from April to November 1989, it made provision for people in three locations: in the transition zone (the southern part of the north and the northern part of the south), in government-held towns in the south, and in the southern countryside increasingly under SPLA control. The needs of southerners displaced to the north were noted but not provided for.

In oblique references to SPLA-held territory, conference papers acknowledged that "Little is known about the dispersed population which has managed to stay in its villages." Yet in a departure from earlier UN assessments which had not mentioned the SPLM/A by name or factored in the needs in its areas, UN officials now included projections of such needs. The plan of action authorized them to deal directly with the insurgents on relief matters.

The conference and its action plan, to which the insurgents soon agreed, succeeded in establishing a framework within which humanitarian needs throughout the entire south could be addressed. Looking back a year later, UN Under-Secretary-General Abdulrahim A. Farah, who played a leading role in negotiating the agreement, summed up its importance as follows: "Lifeline showed the two sides that they were attached to the same umbilical cord. Each side claims assistance for the same people, each is committed to a single Sudan. The Sudan belongs to both."

The Khartoum action plan elicited the consent of both protagonists to the very principles that each had violated so

Dr. John Garang, Chairman of the SPLM,
confers in April 1989 in Kongor with James P. Grant,
Personal Representative of the UN Secretary-General.
UNICEF/Jeremy Hartley

routinely and flagrantly during the years immediately preceding. Humanitarian relief was recognized to be neutral in
character, with access guaranteed to "all civilian non-combatant
populations in need of emergency relief throughout the Sudan."
The government would facilitate assistance efforts in a variety
of ways. Among them was an actively sought concession: UN
and aid agencies associated with Lifeline were granted a more
favorable exchange rate, assuring international funds greater
impact.

Most important, the government agreed to an initial month of
tranquility during which relief efforts could proceed without
fear of military action. In accepting other aspects of the Plan,
the SPLM/A modified this provision to include only specified
"corridors of tranquility" through which safe passage of relief
supplies would be assured. UN officials used their new
authority to negotiate such provisions with the insurgents.

Their intermediary services spared the warring parties face-to-face contact.

The plan of action also laid the groundwork for confusions that would haunt the relief activities launched. The UN assessments of need were very rough and soon had to be adjusted. Tonnage targets of relief supplies to be moved before the rains were virtually impossible to achieve. The conference also contributed to a hard-to-shake confusion about Lifeline itself. Would Lifeline be an umbrella encompassing all relief operations in the southern Sudan, including those already under way? Or would it be a more specific set of activities begun after the conference and carried out by the UN with funds provided to it or through it? While the conference produced agreements between the protagonists and the UN, it did not formalize relationships between the UN and NGOs, the "dirty fingernail people" who would actually deliver many of the goods.

Confusion notwithstanding, the launching of Lifeline helped break a crippling impasse. This was no small accomplishment, even though the hurdles that lay ahead were formidable.

The Wider Context

The humanitarian emergency to which Lifeline responded came toward the end of a decade that had dealt heavy blows to people in the Sudan, throughout the Horn of Africa, and elsewhere on the subcontinent.

The eighties were a time of great hardship for the Sudan, even if the unreliability of data at the national and regional levels makes the extent of the suffering difficult to quantify. Because of poor infrastructure and politicized statistics, even the Sudan's population is not precisely known. Most estimates place the total at about twenty four million, with about eighteen million in the north and six million in the south. Some observers believe, however, that more accurate data would locate as much as half of the Sudanese population in the south. Available evidence suggests that the terms of existence as measured by nutrition, health, and education indicators were even more desperate there than in the north.

Nationwide, the quality of life in one of Africa's poorest countries, never particularly robust, had slipped significantly during the decade, more than offsetting modest gains tallied in the late seventies. The population increased at an average annual rate of 3.1 percent in the eighties, roughly keeping pace with increases in food production. However, for the years through 1987, per capita income lost an average 4.7 percent a year and inflation averaged fully thirty percent annually. The real earnings of civil servants slipped to a small fraction of their levels at the beginning of the decade.[4]

The decade was also a time of tremendous upheaval, particularly with the return of active civil war in 1983. At the time Lifeline was launched, probably a majority of southerners had been displaced. As many as a million and a half people had taken up residence around Khartoum. Several hundred thousand had fled north to camps or rural areas in the transition zone. An unknown number had taken up residence in other rural areas or in towns. At least 500,000 had fled to neighboring countries, primarily Ethiopia.

As the decade progressed, the Sudan's precarious economic situation became of growing concern to international creditors, for the most part Western governments whose point of view was represented by the International Monetary Fund (IMF). In 1985, when the government at the IMF's urging ended subsidies on basic foods and gasoline, strikes and riots followed. The nation's international debt quadrupled during the decade to more than $12 billion. Unfavorable market prices on major Sudanese products such as cotton reduced the Sudan's export earnings. Defense expenditures doubled in the short period between 1984-85 and 1987-88. The Khartoum authorities themselves placed the cost of the war by decade's end at more than $1 million a day. One unpublished analysis of the situation late in the decade concluded that the Sudan's "basic

---

An Aid Worker's Impressions

Working in the southern Sudan is one of the most demanding but rewarding tasks one can imagine. Even if the work be difficult, the time spent in the southern Sudan amongst these proud people will certainly be amongst the most unforgettable memories.

The Nilotic people live a lonely, difficult, and often dangerous life. To survive in a generally hostile environment where nothing is given freely, they have had to develop independence, courage, patience, prudence, and physical as well as mental strength.

They not only move alone through endless and often dangerous wilderness and are thus used to enduring all kinds of hardship. They have also been left alone by history. Neither the English nor the Arabs ever seriously tried to improve their conditions of life or help them to make their first steps into modern times. Really active were only the slave and ivory-traders, who only increased their suspicion for everything unknown, foreign, and thus potentially dangerous.

If one remembers that really nothing good has ever come to the Nilotes from the outside, one may understand the suspicion which sometimes persists even in what concerns the activities of the Red Cross.[5]

Conradin Perner,
International Committee of the Red Cross
March 1989

survival is threatened in the economic, political, institutional, socio-cultural and ecological fields."

Governments that took a dim view of the Sudan's economic policies tightened the screws further during the last half of the decade by reducing or cutting off the flow of outside economic and military aid. A factor contributing to aid reductions was the human rights environment, which became increasingly repressive after 1986.

However serious the provocation, the cutbacks in economic aid probably increased the Sudan's vulnerability to food shortages and famine. They also heightened the importance of humanitarian aid flows, which became the major international resource transfer. The absence of other economic interaction may have reduced international leverage since responses to humanitarian crises from Western governments could be taken more or less for granted. Humanitarian aid was provided in a context of open distrust of the Sudan government and its policies.

The situation in the Sudan was in some respects a microcosm of what was happening during the eighties throughout much of sub-Saharan Africa. The Economic Commission for Africa (ECA) has called the period "Africa's lost decade of development." During the eighties, its Executive Secretary Adebayo Adedeje has reported, "Almost all the gains in human resources development since independence -- notably in school enrollments and health care standards -- have been surrendered."[6]

Of all the world's major regions, observed the World Bank in 1989, "the gravest development problems are in sub-Saharan Africa [where] the combination of slow growth and rapidly expanding populations reduced per capita incomes and left many people close to starvation. Average caloric intake is no higher than twenty years ago."[7] Throughout much of the decade, African nations figured prominently in the monthly

Displaced persons in Narus, southern Sudan in June 1988.
US Committee for Refugees/Morton Hvaal

crop reports of the FAO's Global Information and Early
Warning System. Other long-stayers on the FAO's list included
countries like Ethiopia and Mozambique where, as in the
Sudan, civil strife exacerbated poor food-growing conditions.

At the decade's end, Africa also had the most refugees of any
continent: 4.5 million of fifteen million refugees worldwide.[8]
During the eighties, African borders became increasingly
porous. Mass migrations reflecting civil war, ethnic conflict,
political repression, famine, and poverty propelled people into
neighboring lands. The extent of the displacement was
particularly striking in the Horn. Sudan was host to some
700,000 refugees from four countries, more than 650,000 of
them from Ethiopia. Ethiopia received some 750,000 refugees,
roughly equally divided between Sudanese and Somalis.
Somalia became host to some 350,000 Ethiopians, about the
number of Somalis as had sought refuge in Ethiopia.

"The wars in this region have been going on continuously since 1960," says Bethuel A. Kiplagat, Permanent Secretary of the Kenyan Ministry of Foreign Affairs, "intensifying in the last decade and particularly since 1985." Many Western governments, Kiplagat laments, regard the turmoil in places like the Sudan, Somalia, Ethiopia, and Chad as minor isolated incidents, saying, "Let these people fight among themselves because they are communists, or fundamentalists, or extremists." In Kiplagat's own view, however, "these wars are generating massive civilian casualties. The issues are regional, not local or national," and have international ramifications as well.

Toward the end of the decade the superpowers, whose geopolitical rivalry had fanned the flames of local hostility and fueled regional conflicts, began to use their influence to restrain various protagonists. Reconstruction and reconciliation became possible in southern Africa, Central America, and Afghanistan, with even the situation in Cambodia showing some hopeful signs. At the Washington Summit in May 1990, the US and the Soviet Union also agreed to attempt a joint humanitarian initiative in Ethiopia.

By and large, however, the wars in the Horn have proved more intractable than those that have lent themselves to superpower-blessed mediation. Ethiopia provides territorial access to the SPLA and is believed to offer other support as well, including serving as an arms conduit. The Sudan government aids the insurgents in Eritrea and Tigray. US and Soviet efforts to restrain the protagonists may be complicated by the introduction of Israeli military advisors and materiel into Ethiopia, which threatens to draw the Horn's conflicts into the Arab-Israeli struggle.

Moreover, the riveting resurgence of democracy in Eastern Europe has diverted the attention of Western governments from the ongoing agonies of Africa. Donor governments express a certain "compassion fatigue" in the face of Africa's seemingly endless problems. Civil unrest has made it easier to shift limited aid resources and expertise away from a continent where outside assistance, the stereotype has it, makes little apparent difference. African government officials seem wary of these winds of change from Eastern Europe, though African citizens are finding new hope as more representative institutions begin to take shape across the subcontinent.

In sum, the context for Operation Lifeline Sudan was negative on a variety of fronts. Recurrent economic difficulties in the Sudan during thirty five years of independence were compounded by ineffective political institutions. Six years of war had eroded the quality of life and frustrated efforts to provide assistance. International humanitarian efforts would take place in a climate of distrust of the host government and amid deepening cynicism about Africa's economic doldrums and its slow progress in moving beyond relief. The setting hardly encouraged optimism about Lifeline's chances for success.

Chapter 2
Principle and Action

Lifeline may not have addressed the underlying problems but it did succeed in giving people a ray of hope.

Jennefer Sebstad
Researcher

Lifeline was a struggle, particularly during the early going in April and May 1989. By September it had achieved most of its objectives. It languished from November through March of the following year as the rekindled war slowed relief activities. The warring parties reaffirmed Lifeline's principles in March 1990 and it began to regain some of its momentum in the months that followed.

Overview

Following the Khartoum conference in early March, operations were formally launched during the first week in April with the departure of truck convoys from Khartoum and Nairobi, Kenya for the southern Sudan. (See Appendix A and map, p. 30) Orchestrated by the Secretary-General's Personal Representative James P. Grant, the send-offs were designed to catapult Lifeline onto the international stage, encourage support from governments and the public, and reinforce the commitment of the warring parties.

The media were skeptical. Journalists questioned the attempt to deliver more than 100,000 tons of relief commodities over such a wide and troubled area in a few short months. Their doubts were reinforced by Nairobi-based NGOs, some of them veterans of the southern Sudan. Egil Hagen of NPA in Nairobi labeled Lifeline a publicity stunt.

It took time for Lifeline to hit its stride. The necessary personnel had to be put in place. By mid-April, fifty people had been reassigned from UN offices around the world. A transport system including trucks, planes, barges, railway cars, and engines had to be mobilized. A communications network was needed. The Khartoum plan of action required adaptation to the real world. "We were very much designing this afternoon's step this morning," recalls a UN official at the helm. "Lifeline was instant design, all ad-hoc-racy."

Much of what was accomplished in the early days built on the work of NGOs described in the previous chapter. Such activities included airlifts by a fleet of Red Cross planes to points across the south and by LWF from Nairobi into Juba. Road and river transport encountered frequent delays, with two overland convoys in April and a third in May attacked by unknown armed groups. The first relief train from the north into Bahr el Ghazal was also set upon, jeopardizing its relief mission and threatening the lives of UN personnel on board.

During the first three months, Lifeline edged toward its target of transporting the estimated 107,000 tons of food needed by the end of June. Counting the 13,105 tons in stock and the 16,941 tons moved during March, Lifeline had already attained 22 percent of its target when it officially began in early April. It reached the 39 percent mark by the end of April, 58 percent by the end of May, and 73 percent by the end of June.

Most of the early "hiccups" were out of Lifeline's system by mid-year. Expatriate and indigenous relief personnel were fanning out around the south, assessing needs and monitoring aid distribution. As the rains came and the rivers rose, some areas became less accessible overland and air drops became even more essential. Working relationships among the aid agencies and with the Sudanese authorities improved. No major incidents of harassment were reported. Relief continued to move through five of the eight "corridors of tranquility" agreed to by the warring parties. Beyond food and medicine, deliveries included seeds and tools, human and cattle vaccines, and reconstruction help for local communities. By the end of July the food tonnages had climbed to 78 percent of the target.

Operations became more routine in August and September. A third relief train reached its destinations. The first of three barge convoys made its way up the Nile to Malakal, dropping food in hamlets controlled by either side along the way. Working relationships stabilized further. The UN staff assigned full-time to Lifeline numbered 175 (eighty six from UNICEF, seventy eight from WFP, and eleven from UNDP). Fifty nine staff members were based in Khartoum, directing activities in government-controlled areas. The remaining 116 were based in Kampala and in Nairobi, the command post for Lifeline's southern sector operations.

By the end of September, when James Grant turned over the reins to Michael Priestley, crops were being harvested and aid officials were looking beyond emergency needs to reconstruction and development challenges. The food tonnages had climbed through 88 percent in August to 97 percent at September's end. Lifeline's major logistical chores were largely over, three months later than planned but completed nonetheless. By year's end, some 111,654 tons of food had been transported, topping the 107,000 ton target. Lifeline also transported 3,760 tons of non-food items.

Toward the year's end, military and political developments interrupted this momentum. Lifeline had already survived a military coup at mid-year that deposed Prime Minister Sadiq el Mahdi, with whom Lifeline had been negotiated. The new chief of state, Lieutenant General Omar Hasan al-Bashir, quickly reaffirmed the commitment of his regime to Lifeline's continuation.

With the return of the dry season in September, however, the pause in the fighting from which Lifeline had benefited came under growing duress. In late October, each side accused the other of military actions that brought down the curtain on more than half a year of tranquility. During the lull which had provided a sheltering space for aid activities, crops had been planted, moribund local markets had shown signs of revitalization, and civilian life had begun to return to normal.

When the government closed the Sudan airspace to relief flights in early November, many activities associated with Lifeline were slowed, some halted altogether. A major casualty was the immunization of children against communicable diseases, an effort that had relied on refrigerated vaccines flown to remote areas. Plans to extend Lifeline were stalled for almost five months until, in late March, the warring parties reaffirmed Lifeline's principles and agreed to launch "Lifeline 2."

An initiative as complex as Lifeline needs review from various perspectives. These include establishing humanitarian principle, mobilizing international resources, providing assistance, and strengthening indigenous agencies. The review here focuses on Lifeline activities during 1989.

Establishing the Principle

One of Lifeline's signal accomplishments was to persuade the warring parties to commit themselves publicly to the principle that all civilians have a right to humanitarian assistance, wherever they happen to be located, and that access to them must be assured. Lifeline did not negotiate the breakthrough; the parties had agreed to the principle late the previous year.

Lifeline did place their commitment under an international spotlight, however, and provide them a vehicle for making good on it. As noted earlier, the principle was the same one routinely violated in the years preceding Lifeline.

Even once agreed to, the principle was tested on a day-to-day basis. The right of access of people in need of aid and of aid agencies to them imposed obligations on warring parties and aid agencies alike. The protagonists agreed to provide aid or to allow aid to be provided. In return, they expected aid agencies to demonstrate impartiality (that is, the provision of relief solely on the basis of need), neutrality (the refusal to choose up sides in the conflict), transparency (the non-concealment of relief activities from either party), and accountability.

UN officials stressed the importance of the principle on which Lifeline was built. At a May 1989 press conference in Nairobi, Grant cited agreement between protagonists as one of the twin miracles of Lifeline, the other being the prompt and generous response of donor governments to the UN appeal. The first miracle, he said, formed the basis for one of the decade's biggest relief operations and perhaps one of history's largest interventions in an active civil war.

Some felt that UN officials from the start exaggerated Lifeline's historical importance. Speaking of the involvement of UN personnel in a situation of armed conflict, Harald Schmid de Gruneck of the ICRC observed that "This may have been a premier for the UN." Yet for the ICRC, he noted, whose mandate worldwide is to assist people in just such settings, the Sudan challenge was more routine. In short, the UN was moving with some fanfare into territory better known to others.

Once the principle had been agreed to, relief activities became, in their own right, a means for holding the parties to their

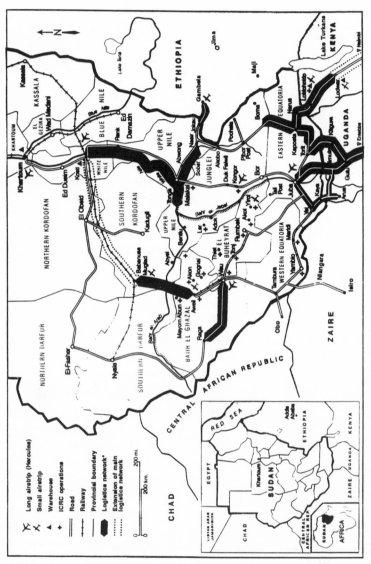

* Logistics networks correspond to corridors of tranquility.

commitment. As Lifeline gathered momentum, the principle became more difficult for either side to violate with impunity. By September, UN officials in New York were noting that "After some five months of successive truces, there are strong pressures on both sides against the resumption of hostilities."

Rekindled war soon proved them wrong. However, the warring parties took pains to distinguish between the resumption of the conflict and any violation of humanitarian principle. In closing airspace to relief flights, government officials said they were not repudiating but rather protecting the principle. (UN officials strongly denied government allegations that Lifeline had transported military items under the guise of relief.) For its part, the SPLA condemned the flight ban itself as a violation of humanitarian principle and accused the government of planning to hold relief hostage to military objectives.

Even early in Lifeline the principle was under constant fire. "The concept of unescorted trains, barges and trucks was recognized as being unprecedented in a civil war zone," reported W. Bryan Wannop, a UN official who organized and then made the harrowing trip in May on the first relief train from Muglad to Aweil.[1] Putting the principle into action meant overcoming the suspicions of those who saw outside assistance as support to the enemy. "Anybody down to the lowest private can stop anything," exclaimed an exasperated NGO official. The object of his wrath was the government, but the insurgents on occasion proved equally intractable.

For their part, aid agencies took care to guard their symbols of humanitarian principle against abuse. Protection was assured within the corridors of tranquility solely to vehicles marked with the Red Cross/Red Crescent symbol or the UN flag, indicating that they were unarmed and carried only humanitarian items. The insignias, however, did not command automatic respect. Some in the north saw the Red Cross symbol as anti-

Muslim. Those who threatened to kill the UN personnel on the Muglad-Aweil train hoped to use the UN flags and Lifeline banners they commandeered as mosquito nets. By and large, however, the insignias helped assure safe passage for relief items and personnel, particularly as the symbols became more familiar sights around the south.

From November 1989 through April 1990, humanitarian principle came under particularly heavy assault, largely but not exclusively from the government side. With the war heating up, "security" restrictions were imposed on aid personnel governing their travel, use of radios, and even authorization to continue programs in the country. The downing of a duly marked relief plane in December (see box, p. 86) represented

---

Sieges and Symbols

The important lesson I've learned from Lifeline is the neutrality point: making it clear to people that you're neutral, favoring neither side. Neutrality really works .... It's more than just your own survival, however. It's a matter of trust and sincerity.

Many times on the river [as relief supplies were being trans-ported], there's been shooting in the air -- to get our attention. We've been told that without the UN flag, we would have been shot at directly.

Marcel R. LeCours, Logistics Monitor, Khartoum

This United Nations flag is fantastic! People in the southern Sudan respect this flag the way they respect their own flag. I am a Colombian. The UN flag is my flag. You are an American. The UN flag is your flag. The flag itself has the world on it. We are all together in that flag. It is us.

Julio Delgado Idarraga, Convoy Leader, Nairobi

a particularly flagrant assault. Less visible pressures were also directed against Sudanese officials involved in Lifeline. In late 1989, the RRC Commissioner was dismissed for having helped draft the new Lifeline agreement. His staff was questioned by security officials about their roles.

Some Lifeline activities, particularly those mounted from Nairobi, continued during these bleak days, relying on the "residual legitimacy" of the Lifeline principle. One major consideration in pressing to launch Lifeline 2, however, was the desire to rescue humanitarian principle and to re-energize lagging relief work. Otherwise, officials feared, Lifeline, begun with a bang, would end with a whimper.

At the donor consultation in Khartoum on March 26, 1990, the government reaffirmed "its commitment to the concept and principles of Operation Lifeline Sudan, including . . . the neutrality of humanitarian relief." The SPLM/A then followed suit, despite dissatisfaction with specific provisions of the new agreement. While affirming that Lifeline "represented a very important principle for humanitarian operations in not only the Sudan but also other conflict situations," SPLM Chairman John Garang lamented the loss of "the unquestionable neutrality of the UN . . . that did the most for the [relief] operation to become a reality."

In short, Lifeline struggled to establish and maintain humanitarian principle against abuse. Generally speaking, it succeeded, thanks in part to the international attention it mobilized to hold the protagonists to their promises. Despite actions that threatened to sabotage the principle altogether, the warring parties never repudiated it. In fact, the review of other aspects of Lifeline tends to bear out the judgment of Svein Tore Rode-Christoffersen of Norwegian Church Aid that "The principle is the best part of Operation Lifeline Sudan."

Mobilizing International Concern

Lifeline took the lead in galvanizing world public opinion, spearheading global fund raising, and providing international presence. In each respect, there were significant accomplishments, offset in part by attendant problems.

First, admirers and detractors alike credit the UN with having put the Sudan crisis on the world map. Throughout much of 1988, the extent of suffering was not widely known beyond relief agency personnel and veteran Sudan watchers. Frenetic NGO efforts to alert constituents and governments failed to turn many heads.

As 1988 progressed, there were signs of growing international awareness. A number of journalists reported first-hand on the devastation in places like Aweil, Abyei, and Muglad, where the displaced were dying of famine and exhaustion in large numbers and children under two were absent altogether. (See photographs, pp. 8, 22 and box, p. 10) During the latter part of the year a series of articles in *The Atlanta Journal and Constitution* by Colin Campbell and Debra Scroggins publicized the widespread killings of southerners by northern militias, deaths in transit camps en route to the north, and even the resurgence of slavery. The August floods attracted international attention to the plight of those who had settled around Khartoum and to the war which propelled them there. The Catholic Fund for Overseas Development (CAFOD), a private British aid group, reported an upsurge in public interest and contributions.

Whatever the level of existing public awareness, Lifeline provided a vehicle for educating the international public about the Sudan crisis. This represented no small accomplishment. "Unheard of conflicts are not of interest to donors," observes an ICRC official. Contributions to such emergencies around the world fluctuate according to the extent to which they become known, not according to the severity of the need. A US State Department official, Jack Davison, believes the public relations aspects of Lifeline -- "the visuals, the dramatizing of the problem" -- were as important as the substantial relief provided. Certainly they were a prerequisite for it.

After the Khartoum conference in March 1989 and the send-offs of the initial convoys in early April, international interest picked up perceptibly. By mid-April, Lifeline was receiving some forty five media inquiries a day. Reporters clamored for more information and an on-the-spot look. Western publics became more aware of the "race against time" as Lifeline hurried to beat the rains. Throughout the middle six months of the year, international coverage of relief activities in the southern Sudan was extensive.

A second major contribution was in global fund raising. Lifeline provided an assessment of needs that was trusted by governments whose information was spotty. SPLA-controlled areas were off limits to officials of other governments and visits to areas controlled by the Sudan government, themselves military targets, involved considerable risk. Since no UN staff other than UNICEF had visited SPLA territory, UN estimates relied heavily on reports from NGOs and the ICRC, whose earlier attempts to sound the alarm had proved unsuccessful.

With the UN imprimatur validating the extremity of the situation, Lifeline became a rallying point for international resource mobilization. Some $78 million was already in hand at the time of the Khartoum conference, largely in the form of food aid responses to the Secretary-General's appeal of late 1988. By the end of May, most of the additional $55 million requested had also been pledged. In June, an additional $48 million was sought. By the end of the year, reports the UN, contributions received by Lifeline totaled some $205 million.

Most of these contributions, whether cash or in-kind, originated with governments. In addition to the $78 million available early in the year, governments provided $62.3 million, including food aid from the US and the EC and aircraft from France, the Federal Republic of Germany, Belgium, and the Netherlands. UN agencies added resources of their own, also originating largely with governments. WFP contributed $21.5 million, UNICEF $17 million, UNDP $3.3 million, and the FAO $250,000.

While Lifeline contributions topped $200 million, total resources available may have reached $300 million. The lower figure does not include major funding received by NGOs either from their own constituencies or from some governments. Additional funds were also raised by the ICRC. The grand total is difficult to determine since many contributions did not go through Lifeline and were not tallied by it. Whatever the total, aid officials have not complained about inadequate resources for the task.

All agencies, whether or not associated with Lifeline, benefited from its resource mobilization efforts. The ICRC, for example, for which funds were requested in the UN appeals, received some $70 million in cash and in-kind support from governments, national Red Cross/Red Crescent societies, and the general public. The ICRC credits Lifeline with having enhanced and reinforced its own fund-raising activities. NGOs, too, believe that sizeable increases in their own levels of receipts during 1989 reflected broader public awareness stimulated by Lifeline. Without Lifeline, such fund raising would have been far less successful.

Lifeline also helped by providing international presence. After a period in which expatriates in the south had been few and far between, Lifeline offered an umbrella under which the vast southern region was opened up to hundreds of international relief workers. The 175 UN personnel assigned full time to

Lifeline were only a portion of a far larger contingent. ICRC activities were staffed by ninety five expatriates, forty one Sudanese from the national Red Cross/Red Crescent society, and 867 locally hired personnel. NGO staff swelled the numbers further still.

The effects of aid personnel were palpable. One UN worker, Patta Smith-Villers, recalls her first visit shortly before Lifeline began to Leer, a small rural community in Upper Nile. "There was a look on people's faces of desolation and shock -- as if years of war and suffering had left them numb with the horror of it all. We saw the same look everywhere we went." On a return visit months later, she said "I had only to think of the change in the look on people's faces to know that the work was worthwhile. People were once again able to smile. We had helped to bring a sense of normality and security just by our presence."

The presence of international personnel also exercised a restraining influence on the protagonists, both in the treatment of civilian populations and in the conduct of the war. "There is no doubt," states the ICRC's Harald Schmid de Gruneck, "that acts of violence by military personnel were deterred by expatriate presence." Both the government and the SPLA conceded as much by denying aid personnel access to areas in which they preferred to have their activities remain un-observed.

At a number of points during Lifeline 2 as well, UN officials sought to use their good offices on behalf of Sudanese civil-ians. When government authorities in mid-1990 began the major task of relocating the many displaced persons from around Khartoum back to the areas in Bahr el Ghazal from which they had come, UN officials sought to assure that adequate preparations had been made and that those who were involved were being relocated voluntarily. Lifeline staff also worked actively to discourage the SPLA from the continued use of child soldiers.

* * *

UN contributions to the relief of suffering through mobilizing world opinion, generating resources, and providing international presence were substantial. In each area, however, problems undercut the full effectiveness of Lifeline's efforts.

First, its success in galvanizing world public opinion had negative features as well. In the view of some in the media and among NGOs, Lifeline created a theatrical atmosphere which detracted from the serious task of delivering relief. The convoy send-offs, they said, were more symbolic than real. Photo-opportunities for UNICEF Goodwill Ambassador Audrey Hepburn, helpful in putting the Sudan crisis on the international map, involved trade-offs in the use of staff time and aircraft space.

UN officials take a longer view, noting that Lifeline was about more than logistics. Lifeline's use of the media, they maintain, illustrates how the international community can be enlisted in the support of life-saving initiatives. Flagging off the trucks was largely symbolic, explains UNICEF's Khartoum representative Farid Rahman, but the food eventually did reach the south overland in large quantities. Sending off the train from Muglad did not open the railroad, but four trains eventually did get through. And while the departure ceremony for the barges was a token gesture, the Nile was eventually opened to relief traffic.

UN information management drew fire on another count. Lifeline officials, viewing Western media as their gateway to European and North American publics and resources, did not give high priority to cultivating Sudanese, Kenyan, and other Arab and African media. As a result, the significance of what was taking place was largely lost on those publics and Lifeline missed an opportunity to create a needed non-Western constituency. Suspicions of Lifeline as a foreign intervention driven by Western political interests were reinforced.

A third criticism concerns Lifeline's data. Compiled hurriedly in the interests of speeding the relief task, the UN figures proved not altogether reliable. For the UN no less than for governments, insurgent-held territory had been *terra incognita.* As in other civil conflicts where the UN has had difficulty developing sound data independently of the host government, its involvement proved, in the words of one UN official, "a voyage of discovery."

Moreover, the data were used to frame objectives primarily in terms of tonnages and transport. The ton soon took on a life of its own, more political and polemical than nutritional in nature. An overemphasis on the tonnages moved, observed a consultant visiting the south in May 1989, "has tended to create a short-term relief mentality that obscures equally important medium-term needs and the opportunity to provide relief in a way that supports, rather than undercuts, longer-term development." Important but less tangible benefits of the relief effort received short shrift.

Defending Lifeline figures as the best possible in difficult circumstances, one UN official observes that "In the kingdom of the blind, the one-eyed man is king." In the rocky terrain of civil wars, however, the one-eyed may well stumble. UN officials acknowledge in retrospect that less emphasis on tonnage targets might also have avoided the continuing impression that Lifeline was losing the race and might have directed more attention to its other accomplishments.

Fund-raising success also masked a more fundamental problem. Was Lifeline a structure for managing a clearly identified set of activities to meet the needs articulated in the Khartoum plan of action? Or was it an umbrella for a wider range of activities, over some of which the UN itself would have little control? Estimates of Lifeline resources range between $135 million and $300 million, depending on what is included. Confusion about the nature and identity of Lifeline resulted in problems of coordination and accountability examined later in the chapter.

In broader perspective, the very effectiveness of Lifeline's mobilization was something of a problem. Praising Lifeline for its successful fund raising, WFP Executive Director James C. Ingram observes that at the same time other urgent human needs elsewhere were receiving little attention. Lifeline came to reflect "a certain inequity" in the deployment of the world's limited attention and resources. While Ingram's observation is not directed at Lifeline in its own right, it suggests that the international system for responding to major emergencies, currently dependent on high-visibility efforts to put a single country on the map, needs to be placed on a surer and more universal footing.

Finally, while the value of international aid personnel is undisputed, Lifeline is criticized for the staff it provided. The UN, some say, imported Westerners without prior experience in the region when knowledgeable Africans were available. The problem was not unique to the UN. Other aid agencies, too, had difficulty finding informed expatriates, many of whom were unavailable or reluctant to expose themselves to the hardships of the Sudan. UN officials point out in their own defense that while mistakes may have been made, at least 90 percent of Lifeline's staff was hired from the region.

Here as in other key Lifeline decisions there were unavoidable trade-offs. Hiring locally available persons was quicker and cheaper, produced staff more knowledgeable about local realities, and raised fewer anxieties among the political authorities. Outside experts, however, knew the workings of the aid agencies better and brought with them an added international dimension and experience from crises elsewhere.

Delivering the Goods

In addition to mobilizing international concern, Lifeline delivered aid. What was accomplished in its relief operations? How well were they coordinated? Were its resources used wisely?

Foremost among Lifeline's accomplishments was its provision of food. Before the year's end, some 111,654 metric tons of commodities had been contributed to the southern Sudan. The major donors were the EC, which provided 60,490 tons, and the US, which provided 40,650 tons.

Arranging transport for the commodities donated was a major logistical challenge and accomplishment. As noted earlier, trucks, railroad cars, barges, and aircraft were pressed into service. During the ten months beginning in March 1989, a total of some 98,500 tons were moved; the balance had already been transported in January and February. The prime movers were the NGOs, who transported an estimated 52,000 tons, slightly over half of the total. UN agencies moved 33,000 tons and the ICRC 12,500. (See photographs, pp. 43, 50, and 143)

Distribution, the final step in the chain, included by year's end some 89,750 tons. Most active at this point in the process were NGOs, who saw some 52,000 tons, or 58 percent of the total, to final destinations. Also involved were UN agencies (10,500 tons), the ICRC (8,250 tons), and Sudanese relief committees (19,000 tons). At the end of December, 21,900 tons remained in stock and available for distribution in early 1990.

Roughly three-quarters of the food went to people in government-controlled areas, the rest to people in SPLA territory. With some ninety percent of the land area of the south controlled by the SPLA, the division seemed lopsided. However, large concentrations of people in the government-held garrison towns of Juba, Wau, and Malakal needed food and, unlike those in the countryside, could not grow enough to meet their own needs.

The food was primarily cereal grains, with smaller amounts of vegetables, oils, and, for vulnerable groups, protein-rich processed foods. There is general agreement that most of the food reached the intended beneficiaries. Some "leakage" took place, however, probably more in the early months than after an extensive network of monitors had been deployed to keep tabs on deliveries. The extent to which soldiers benefited will be examined in the following chapter.

Based on detailed field reports, WFP officials who handled Lifeline's food aid component estimate that some 1.5 million persons received food. While they do not claim that Lifeline saved as many lives as were lost during 1988, they note that 1989 was a year without starvation in the south. The warring parties concur. (See photographs, pp. 69, 111)

Of course, improved climate, meteorological and political alike, made for better harvests. However, Lifeline food can take considerable credit for helping avoid a repeat of the previous year. Nutrition surveys in late 1989 and in 1990 confirmed widespread nutritional improvement, although in certain localized areas there remained reason for concern -- and for continuing supplementary rations for vulnerable groups.

Food aid did more, however, than feed people through general food distribution or special programs for pregnant women, infants, and young children. On many occasions, its arrival caused local food prices to drop. More affordable prices benefited the population as a whole, whether or not individuals themselves received relief commodities. Food aid played a significant role in overcoming what observers had termed "the near total collapse of the rural economy in the south."

Despite the attention riveted on Lifeline's food component, non-food items may in the long run have brought more durable benefits. The 3,760 tons of non-food items paled by comparison with far larger tonnages of food. Expenditures on non-food items also commanded a smaller share of Lifeline's total budget. Yet their impacts were substantial. Activities managed from UNICEF's Khartoum office in government-controlled areas alone are estimated to have benefited over one million persons. Major items transported included agricultural hand tools, seeds, medicines, and shelter materials.

To speed relief, the British government donated a heavy vehicle ferry to WFP which was flown to Nairobi, transported overland to the Nile in Uganda, assembled, and deployed.
WFP/Jeff Share

Non-food programs were budgeted at $17 million in 1989. The resources contributed by ten governments were amplified by funds mobilized from the general public by eleven national citizen's committees for UNICEF. The activities underwritten were, in order of their decreasing share of UNICEF's budget, water supplies and sanitation, immunization, primary health care and essential drugs, nutrition and supplementary feeding, and food production.

Increasing water supplies was a major contribution by Lifeline since access to potable water had been a prime casualty of the war. Lifeline activities included rehabilitating hand pumps and bore holes and installing new equipment, providing water and constructing water yards, and supplying fuel and equipment for generating power to supply water. Beneficiaries in government-controlled areas alone are reported in the hundreds of thousands. (See photograph, p. 58)

Lack of immunization had been a major cause of death among children during 1988. (See box, p. 10) An expanded program of immunization therefore became a priority. In SPLA-controlled areas, shots had been given by November 1989 to more than 115,000 children against measles, polio, diphtheria, and tuberculosis and to 30,000 women of child-bearing age against tetanus toxoid. The tally was only slightly lower in government-controlled areas. The numbers of beneficiaries were steadily increasing until the ban on relief flights interrupted activities in November 1989. (See box, p. 96)

Other accomplishments in the health sector were also sizeable. Five years of war had decimated the health system in a region that even before the war had known some of the world's highest rates of mortality and morbidity among children and women. UNICEF provided essential drugs, trained health personnel, and upgraded health facilities. UNDP strengthened the Ministry of Health's work in government-controlled areas.

Food production activities improved food security considerably. UNICEF provided some 480 tons of seeds to cultivators in SPLA-controlled areas, an amount which, with good growing conditions, could produce fully half of Lifeline's total 1989 food aid tonnage. The FAO provided agricultural inputs and supplies. UNICEF also made available thousands of agricultural hand tools and limited numbers of fishing nets and fishhooks. Tens of thousands of cattle vaccinations were carried out, sometimes opening the way to vaccinating people, and vice versa. (See photograph, p. 148)

Food production and livestock herds rebounded in 1989, as did people's general nutritional health. Lifeline plans in 1990 call for lower food tonnages and even greater emphasis on agricultural inputs. SPLA-controlled areas alone are to receive 1900 tons of seeds and 500,000 agricultural hand tools, a shift corresponding to what the people themselves want. A 1989 WFP report found that the Sudanese place a higher value on such agricultural assistance than on food commodities. Since waiting to be fed is a social stigma for many Africans, movement toward agricultural self-reliance contributed to a rebirth of dignity.

In delivering the goods, Lifeline proved able to adapt its plans and strategies as the situation warranted, building on what worked and setting aside what did not. While Lifeline deserves praise for its flexibility and ability to improvise, its lack of contingency planning proved a definite weakness.

* * *

How well were Lifeline's activities coordinated? Governments give Lifeline high marks. NGOs offer mixed reviews. The UN itself is divided.

Donor governments are for the most part strongly positive in their views of Lifeline's service delivery and coordination. "Lifeline realized its main objective," says a Dutch government official: to get food into the south and avoid starvation. "It's a terrific achievement in political and historical terms," says his British counterpart. EC officials are also enthusiastic. The EC had a special interest in coordination, having provided more than half of the food during 1989 through WFP, ICRC, NGOs, and the Sudanese relief authorities: on the government's side the Relief and Resettlement Commission (RRC) and for the insurgents, the Sudan Relief and Rehabilitation Association (SRRA).

The sheer number of aid agencies involved -- intergovernmental, governmental, and non-governmental -- made coordination essential. In a given region where aid was being provided, there might be at one time or another officials from UNICEF and WFP, international and Sudanese NGOs, the ICRC, and the RRC or SRRA. Officials from countries such as the Netherlands, Sweden, Italy, and the Federal Republic of Germany were also occasional visitors.

In the Kapoeta area in SPLA-controlled southeastern Equatoria, for example, an array of agencies, activities, and funding sources were involved during Lifeline. They included World Vision International, with programs in seed distribution, cattle vaccination, and the supply of medicines; the International Rescue Committee, assisting with supplementary feeding, immunization, and community health worker training; and the Comité Internationale Medicale pour l'Urgence et Developpement (MEDIC), doing well drilling and hand pump maintenance in collaboration with Lutheran World Relief.

Also active were the African Medical and Research Foundation, with programs of training in the health field; Street Kids International, in education; Assistance Medicale Internationale (AMI), in primary health care; and Oxfam-US in agriculture.

The funders included UNICEF, AID and other bilateral aid agencies, and of course NGOs themselves. UN officials estimate that from these activities most of the roughly 250,000 civilians in the Kapoeta area benefited.

If governments were generally positive regarding Lifeline's coordinating work, NGOs were more divided. The difficulty was not created by competition: there was more than enough work for everyone to do. The problem first surfaced when Lifeline claimed "credit" for tonnages of commodities moved by NGOs. The UN reasoned that such food was directed toward needs identified in the Khartoum plan of action. The food and much of its transport cost had been provided by the same governments that supported Lifeline directly. Why should NGO activities not "count" toward Lifeline's targets?

Some NGOs took a different view. They had provided relief well in advance of Lifeline, had made their own arrangements with governments for commodities and transport, and had augmented government contributions with support from their own contributors. Nor had they been fully consulted by UN officials as Lifeline was being planned and its implementation discussed. With Lifeline's targets framed in terms of transport and Lifeline officials taking NGO cooperation for granted, their altogether critical role in distribution received little attention.

"Credit" is hardly the driving force behind humanitarian activity, though it does have a bearing on the scale of funds agencies are able to raise. Even had UN officials been more collegial toward NGOs, however, there might well have been a problem. Underlying the dispute was a strong NGO desire to retain a certain independence.

Many NGOs were appreciative of UN efforts in facilitating and enhancing their work. "Lifeline improved our efficiency," says Bruce Miller, head of the Sudan delegation of the League of

Red Cross and Red Crescent Societies. His agency benefited from UN support in logistics and communication. "We need the UN and the UN needs us," another NGO observes. A third notes that "Lifeline has helped us maintain access to people in the south." Clearly there were many indispensable functions for the UN, but coordinating NGO relief efforts may not have been one of them.

Appreciation notwithstanding, some NGOs viewed the UN as structurally biased in favor of its member governments. Under normal circumstances, this might not present a particular problem. However, in a situation of civil war in which a UN member state is a protagonist, lack of UN impartiality may undermine the viability of the aid provided. If, as one NGO put it rather dramatically, "The UN can be shut down by Khartoum any time they want," the association of NGOs with Lifeline may expose NGO work to added political pressure.

The difficulties experienced by the UN before Lifeline in providing aid and protecting UN staff in the exercise of their humanitarian functions underscored the concern. Moreover, as NGOs had sought to launch their own programs in SPLA areas in 1988, UNICEF, also reflecting in part pressure from donor governments, had pressed them to hold off until the Sudan government had agreed to allow UN programs to proceed.

"Let not the bias of the UN," says Dan Kelly, executive director of ACROSS, "be the means of frustrating or constraining NGOs, which need not have that bias themselves." Kelly acknowledges Lifeline's value in fighting for principle and opening humanitarian space. However, affiliation with Lifeline, he believes, would expose NGOs to pressure from the government, and, for that matter, from the SPLM/A. For Lifeline to seek to coordinate NGO work, and for governments to expect it to do so, was bound to encounter difficulties.

Finally, Lifeline was not particularly effective in coordinating the work of UN agencies themselves. "Lifeline" was not a structural entity but an ad-hoc creation, designed for a brief two- or three-month period. It was a center of energy linking UN agencies involved in the Sudan, not a command post with clear lines of authority and accountability.

Unlike the UN's Office of Emergency Operations for Africa in the 1984-85 famine, Lifeline was not an organizational unit with authority to formulate and assure common policies and strategies among UN agencies. It was a temporary home for some dedicated international civil servants detailed for short stints who remained accountable throughout to their own agencies, to which they would shortly return.

A second problem was that individual UN agencies brought to the common effort their own institutional styles. The major players were UNICEF, WFP, and UNDP. The FAO and the UN Disaster Relief Organization (UNDRO) were involved only at the margin. The UN High Commissioner for Refugees (UNHCR) was not in the picture at all since Lifeline assisted only people displaced within their own country, not refugees present in the Sudan from other countries.

With a long tradition of working amid civil strife and with NGOs, UNICEF brought flexibility and an action orientation to its involvement in Lifeline. Administrative, personnel, and budget decisions were quickly made at the beginning of Lifeline and the UNICEF staff was off and running. UNICEF soon established its own sub-offices in SPLA-controlled territory. Once emergency needs were brought under control, UNICEF staff began planning for and carrying out reconstruction and even quasi-development activities.

WFP, which enjoyed better working relationships with NGOs as Lifeline began, was less aggressive, less flexible in coping

Much of Lifeline's food was moved overland. This truck leads
a UN convoy proceeding south from Khartoum
and is identified by the UN flag.
UNICEF/Jeremy Hartley

with the exigencies of the civil war, and more dependent for
decision-making on its Rome headquarters. WFP took longer
to gear up for action, relied on mobile personnel rather than
setting up field offices, and essentially withdrew from SPLA-
controlled areas once the logistical challenges had been met.

True to its own worldwide mission and style, UNDP dealt
primarily with government ministries in the capital. An agency without a history of extensive involvement in internal armed
conflicts, UNDP gave valuable help to various Khartoum
ministries, lent technical assistance in emergency preparedness
and response, and provided air transport for assessment and
relief activities. UNDP also outstationed a representative in
government-controlled Juba who coordinated UN activities and
played a creative intermediary role between NGOs and
government authorities.

UNDP headed up the UN's emergency operation in the Sudan before Lifeline and contributed a highly respected senior official to manage Lifeline after James Grant's departure. Michael Priestley's strengths too lay in dealing with the Khartoum authorities. Unlike UNICEF, the UNDP's office in Nairobi was not much involved in Lifeline, even after UNDP assumed overall responsibility for the program.

The appointment of Grant to head Lifeline accentuated these inter-agency differences. Since he continued as UNICEF Director and committed the institutional resources of his agency to Lifeline's needs, Lifeline quite naturally reflected UNICEF's approach to operations and fund raising. The fact that Grant headed a relief effort the major component of which was food was something of an anomaly.

Inter-agency differences, while harmonized a bit, were never really resolved. The idea that "emergencies force the UN to act effectively as a system," rightly concludes an unpublished evaluation by a donor government, "cannot be confirmed on the basis of Operation Lifeline Sudan." Basic decisions about program objectives, funding, media, and reporting were seldom reached through collegial inter-agency discussions. As a result, information remains far less readily available about Lifeline as a whole than about the activities of a given UN agency. The agencies themselves acknowledge these problems and are seeking to address them.

* * *

Finally, were Lifeline's resources used wisely? Lifeline was without doubt an expensive program. Its high cost reflected the geography of the southern Sudan, the existence of the civil war, and the lateness of the hour. People needing relief were scattered across a wide landscape barely connected by roads, many of which were passable only during the dry season.

Hostilities often made the shortest distance between two points longer, insurance costs higher, and "incentive payments" necessary. Launching the operation a month or two before the rains forced heavy use of air transportation. The SPLA's insistence that none of the relief bound for its areas be transported from Khartoum added time and expense.

"Yes, it was a very costly operation," concedes Ulf Kristoffersson, who coordinated it from UNICEF headquarters in New York. "Logistics obstacles are what made the program costly. There would be no starvation anywhere in Africa if we had access to the people." The costs would have been even higher, officials contend, had Lifeline not done its best to contain them -- for example, by hiring most of its staff from the region and purchasing maize from nearby Kenya and Uganda and sorghum from the northern Sudan.

The intensive monitoring insisted upon by donor governments also drove costs up. "There has never been a relief operation as carefully reported," states Peter Jobber, WFP representative in Khartoum and a veteran of the Cambodian relief operation of 1979-80 and of Bangladesh following the 1984 floods. "The UN had at a given time in the field twenty seven official UN staff and eight or nine additional staff wearing UN arm bands checking on food deliveries. This presence represented an order of magnitude larger than that used for monitoring most large emergency programs. It was needed to ensure delivery of relief supplies without diversion."

Lifeline was also expensive because it underwrote the costs of activities benefiting the wider aid community. Regular Lifeline flights were expensive, but they transported NGO and donor government personnel and supplies throughout the south. Lifeline's initial investment of $336,000 in the base camp at Lokichoggio in northern Kenya seemed excessive, even before monthly operating costs of $46,000. Yet "Loki" became a useful logistical and communications resource for personnel from all aid agencies coming from and going to the Sudan.

Granted Lifeline was expensive, was its cost excessive? The question is really "excessive" in relation to what. It is difficult to find bench marks against which Lifeline expenditures may be set. The problem is in part the uniqueness of the Sudan situation and in part the absence of adequate comparative data. While difficult to answer within the limitations of the current study, the essential questions can at least be framed.

Was Lifeline's cost excessive compared with other major international relief programs? The UN's initiative in Cambodia and along the Thai border in the late seventies had a comparable civil strife setting but not the immense distances of the Sudan to contend with. Flood relief in Bangladesh in 1984 confronted massive need but without the civil war component. Ethiopian famine in 1984-85 had logistics and distance problems but less of an intrusive war. There were also parallels to UN relief efforts in Mozambique and Somalia but again with variations in scale and degrees of difficulty.

"It has proved far more difficult to work in the Sudan than in other major international relief programs such as Biafra, Thailand, and Ethiopia," observes Nils Enqvist. Head of WFP's Nairobi office, Enqvist is a veteran of many humanitarian assistance and peacekeeping operations.

Were the costs of UN programs substantially larger than similar activities operated by NGOs? Since UN and NGO activities were running side-by-side in the same areas, the comparison should be easy. UNICEF estimates the cost of immunizations at $30 per child, WFP the cost of food aid through Lifeline at $150 per person. Comparable data, however, are not readily available from NGOs. While NGOs are widely assumed to do things more economically, they may also compute costs differently. Nor do their calculations reflect their savings from services provided by the UN.

As regards comparisons of administrative overhead, NPA calculates overhead costs at 1.4 percent of its total budget, a fraction of UNICEF's 12 percent or WFP's 14 percent for personnel and administration. Each figure, however, needs analysis. Is the cost of a Land Rover or of monitoring staff considered part of "overhead" or of "program?" Do the overhead figures compared include fund raising and communications costs? UNICEF reports administrative costs in the Sudan of half its costs in the UN relief operation in Afghanistan, which suggests that it has run a tight ship. That, too, would require further review.

Were expenditures by Lifeline for transport, perhaps the single largest component, excessive? Here again, simple comparisons may be misleading. UNICEF reports having spent 14.05 percent of its Sudan budget on logistics, including monitoring. WFP's percentage, which is considerably higher, includes major amounts for handling and storage, the upgrading of roads and landing strips, and the purchase and maintenance of rail cars. The ICRC reports lower expenditures of 4.27 percent on operational support. Given the particulars, the *highest* percentage might well represent the most cost-effective investment in transport.

Expenditures for air transport, Lifeline's most expensive item and its most criticized, do not lend themselves to easy scrutiny either. An estimated forty percent of Lifeline's food commodities moved by air, largely due to the return of the rainy season. Yet it is difficult to determine whether the figure could have been much lower or whether, within air transport expenditures, substantial economies could have been realized.

Delivering relief by a Twin Otter plane with space for less than a ton of cargo was far more expensive per ton than by a 20-ton payload Hercules C-130, but there were many places the larger planes could not land. Moving a ton of cargo from Khartoum to Malakal cost $850 by air as contrasted with $110 by river, yet barges were not working when people were desperately hungry. Delivering a ton to more remote areas was more expensive than to people nearer at hand, but also more urgent. Transporting a ton from Khartoum to Wau or Aweil by air cost from $1200 to $2400, depending upon the season, the military situation, the amount of insurance, and the safety precautions. Stated costs sometimes reflected the actual cost paid by Lifeline, sometimes the more arbitrary value assigned by various governments donating the aircraft.

Determining whether such costs were excessive would also require taking into account the nature of the item transported, how urgently it was needed, whether other transport means were available, and whether good use was made of it upon arrival. As a result, the average cost of WFP air shipments of $844 per ton is not necessarily more justifiable than the higher average costs incurred by ICRC or UNDP. Nor does it follow that average WFP road transport costs of $200-300 per ton were excessive despite lower costs paid by some NGOs. The average cost per ton by NPA of $160 per ton may have been the best bargain around, but establishing that, too, would take additional analysis.

Costs also need to be judged in relation to accomplishments. The question is not whether the average transport cost of food was high but whether it was justified by the benefits achieved. Items transported may have brought gains well beyond the nutritional, medical, or agricultural value of the goods themselves. If Lifeline strengthened the capacity of local institutions to deal with present and future challenges, or represented an investment in peace (the subject of a later chapter), this, too, should be factored into cost-benefit calculations. At the aggregate level, Lifeline's $200 million in 1989 represented about half of the Sudan government's war-related expenditures for six months.

In short, it is difficult to judge whether Lifeline, an expensive program at either $200 or $300 million, used resources as wisely as possible. Whether or not major economies could have been made, transport costs, like commodities themselves, represent a smaller share of Lifeline's 1990 budget. Air transport in particular is likely to loom less large given firmer policy favoring surface transport and more established and competitive rates among air carriers. Whatever a more detailed review of 1989 may eventually conclude, Lifeline promises to be more economical the second time around.

Strengthening Sudanese Capacity

To what extent did Lifeline's activities strengthen the capacity of indigenous Sudanese institutions to cope with emergencies? Here Lifeline did not acquit itself particularly well, and for a number of reasons.

First, emergencies in developing countries involve a built-in tension between avoiding starvation, which requires immediate action, and strengthening local institutions to do the job themselves, a longer term process. Saving lives takes quick action; capacitation is slower. "It's not easy to collaborate with local institutions and people," says an aid practitioner in Khartoum, "and you can always use the excuse that emergency needs forced you to do the job yourself. But that remains an excuse."

Second, Lifeline did not claim to be about capacitation. A short-term intervention begun in April, it was expected to be over by September. Its plan of action did commit the government to strengthen the RRC, establish local relief committees, and facilitate relief activities in other ways. The granting of a more favorable exchange rate alone, General Bashir points out, represented a government contribution of some ninety million Sudanese pounds. Yet the idea of Lifeline as a partnership was never really articulated.

Should Lifeline be faulted for not doing something it did not set out to do? In historical perspective, yes. Relief operations in 1984-86, when thirty-five million people in some twenty drought-stricken African countries were at risk, were sharply criticized for having failed to develop local capacity. The experience of the Sudan famine of mid-decade should have assured higher priority in 1989 to local institution-building.

The issue is, in fact, a structural one. "Given the risk of the political and/or military manipulation of relief assistance," observes Gayle Smith, a critic of the use of traditional relief strategies when the cause of a famine is war, "donors are inclined to play a more dominant role and to scrutinize aspects of a relief operation that might, in peacetime, go unmonitored. The consequence is often that little or no effort is made to increase local capacity to manage disasters. In the Horn of Africa, where continued conflict and drought guarantee the recurrence of famine, it is imperative that local populations be empowered to manage the crisis. Otherwise, a dangerous dependency will set in and the need for external intervention will increase rather than decrease."

Third, donor governments by 1989 had lost patience with Khartoum and were committed to providing only short-term assistance and nothing beyond. In the years between the famines, they had become so exasperated with the government's economic, military, and human rights policies that they had cut off almost all non-emergency aid. They approached the 1989 challenge as one of helping people *despite* their government. "Donor governments were forever saying, 'We don't trust the Sudan government,'" recalls an observer. "'We won't send any food unless the NGOs are involved.'" Most NGOs themselves viewed the government as obstacle rather than partner. Suspicions of the policies of the insurgents ran almost equally deeply.

While the frustrations were understandable, the resulting policy was not altogether consistent. First, the distinction between emergency assistance and longer-term aid was somewhat arbitrary. General Bashir had logic on his side in observing that

"the donor countries are not forthcoming in helping us to increase our local food productivity. With a little assistance, we could produce enough food for displaced persons within the Sudan, refugees from other countries, and even send food to our neighbors." Indeed, why not help the Sudan toward greater self-reliance?

Second, it seemed contradictory to profess humanitarian concern for people and then, because of reservations about their government's

Lifeline provided potable water to villages and towns.
UNICEF/Mariantonietta Peru

economic, military, or human rights policies, to deny them non-emergency aid. "Should development assistance be linked to the human rights records of the recipient country?", asks Thorvald Stoltenberg, UN High Commissioner for Refugees. "It may be tempting to say yes. But why should people in need be denied help because of their government's poor human rights record? That would make their situation even worse."[2]

There was some truth, of course, to the view that development could not be pursued and Sudanese capacities meaningfully strengthened as long as the civil war itself continued. However, during most of 1989, when the south was not the scene of active hostilities, there was indeed space for assistance of a more durable sort. Even after the rekindled war had injected new uncertainty about the future, UNICEF and NGOs were managing to provide useful non-emergency assistance. More such aid might have considerably enhanced Sudanese self-reliance.

A fourth reason why Lifeline did not do more to strengthen indigenous capacity was that counterpart institutions themselves were weak and otherwise inclined. Lifeline's formal points of contact were the RRC and the SRRA. Both had been established at mid-decade to deal with international aid donors. The SRRA in particular was hobbled by a lack of leadership and technical capacity. "When Lifeline started out," observed one SRRA official a year later, "the SRRA's Agricultural Coordinator didn't have a desk or a chair, a paper or a pen."

During Lifeline, substantial efforts were made to strengthen both entities. The EC seconded staff to the RRC, which also received funding from donor governments. UNICEF, governments, and NGOs also provided funds, vehicles, management training, and other support to the SRRA. The SRRA in particular made significant progress. "Our emphasis in Lifeline," says Vincent E. O'Reilly, coordinator of Lifeline's southern sector, "has been to ensure that at the end of the operation, we would have built and left in place a capacity among the population and our counterparts to sustain the programs of rehabilitation." In fact, as the SPLA consolidated control over the south, the SRRA came to discharge its civil administration responsibilities more effectively. In 1990 it carried out joint surveys of food needs with Lifeline and became a more accountable aid partner, even while claiming that its progress had been made in spite of Lifeline rather than because of it.

But there were countervailing political forces. The RRC's

political base was not strong enough to give it much freedom of operation and, as emergency resources flowed into the country, more powerful ministries came to resent being bypassed. Substantial EC funds offered to the RRC failed to receive the approval of other ministries, which during the Bashir regime seem to have been strengthened as counterweights.

For its part, the SRRA was integral to the SPLM, staffed by decommissioned SPLA officers and

A monitor tallies food supplies.
UNICEF/Mariantonietta Peru

serving the political objectives of the insurgency. "If Lifeline has done anything," says O'Reilly, "it has helped create a confidence in the SRRA which may help it distance itself from the army and actually deal with community needs." The realistic optimum in this regard, however, is greater SRRA functional autonomy, not full independence from the political movement it will continue to serve.

Fifth, while problems of developing effective working relationships with the RRC and the SRRA led to a larger role for NGOs, Lifeline showed a clear preference for international over indigenous NGOs. "International NGOs had a separate track to the UN," notes one Sudanese observer with some bitterness. Individual donor governments also had a clear preference for NGOs based in their own country, and those NGOs themselves were not fully committed to strengthening their Sudanese counterparts.

While not in a position to bear the full financial costs, Sudanese NGOs could clearly have played a more major role in Lifeline-associated activities, short of shouldering the entire operational burden. Groups like the SCC, Sudanaid, the Sudanese Red Crescent Society, and the Islamic African Relief Agency (IARA) had pressed relief efforts well in advance of Lifeline. "As an indigenous agency very much involved in humanitarian work," IARA's Director General Dr. Abdalla Suliman El Awad rightly observes, "we should have been allowed a larger share in Lifeline's activities."

The absence of Sudanese and particularly Muslim NGO involvement underscored the Western and Christian nature of Lifeline. "One of the sad things," muses General Bashir as he reflects on the relief effort, "is that up to now, the West and the white man still believe that they are trustees of us in the Sudan and in Africa. We believe that we're mature enough and understand our problems and how to solve them better than anyone else." The limited partnership established with indigenous NGOs forfeited points of contact with the Sudanese government and public and perhaps with other Arab and Muslim governments and publics as well.

The failure of aid agencies to tap local NGO resources repeated a major mistake from the earlier Sudan famine. One recommendation made in 1986, following a review of relief in the Sudan and elsewhere, was that "the value of local organizations needs to be recognized by their own governments and international organizations" and their capacity strengthened.[3] International NGOs share the blame for not having done so with the UN and governments. "The NGOs have a lot to answer for," notes one close observer of the Khartoum scene, "especially in their failure to 'Sudanize' their organizations." In fairness, some NGOs, particularly those in non-food activities, did seek to enlist and assist indigenous counterparts.

In short, Lifeline receives mixed reviews regarding its strengthening of local institutions to cope with the 1989 emergency and future humanitarian and development challenges. It was least successful in its dealings with the Sudan government, which, feeling excluded from relief activities, moved to reassert its prerogatives in 1990. It did more to facilitate the development of the SRRA although ongoing problems remained. Neither Lifeline nor agencies associated with it did much to enhance the contribution or effectiveness of Sudanese NGOs.

Had capacitation been a major objective, it is likely that indigenous institutions could have been strengthened without slowing the pace of relief activities unduly. Such an approach would have left the Sudan better positioned to meet future emergencies more nearly on its own.

* * *

If Lifeline had not been on the scene, would the humanitarian situation have been more perilous? The answer is clearly yes. Improved weather in 1989 over 1988 itself eased the danger. However, Lifeline may indeed take major credit for the upsurge in aid activities that helped avert a repetition of the experience of the previous year.

Lifeline deserves high praise for having established and preserved humanitarian principle in extremely difficult circumstances. It mobilized a large-scale international response and helped assure that relief supplies reached those in need, even with problems of coordination and even at considerable expense. It did less well in facilitating indigenous involvement in the process.

As it raced against the clock, Lifeline was judged primarily by tonnages moved or not moved. Ultimately, however, it should be judged in larger compass. "We've averted a repeat of the famine," says Vincent O'Reilly in summing up. "Yet Lifeline was not about the relief commodities moved but about peace, almost an accidental by-product." Lifeline's relation to peace and to the politics of the protagonists is the subject of upcoming chapters. There too, the reviews are somewhat mixed.

Chapter 3
Relief and Politics

The problem is not of morality versus politics but rather of the kind of politics which allow moral restraints to emerge and be observed.[1]

Independent Commission
on International Humanitarian Issues

Politics pervaded Lifeline from its inception.   Lifeline was required because the Sudan's political institutions had failed to meet people's needs.   Political objectives and choices resulted in military strategies that exacted an enormous human toll. Political considerations led the warring parties to agree to Lifeline and affected the ways they allowed it to be implemented.   Lifeline, in turn, had political ramifications for their relationship.

Politics did not stop with the protagonists, however.   Political factors influenced decisions by governments, the UN, and NGOs concerning whether to help, when, how much, and through what channels.   The aid agencies themselves, even those disavowing political agendas, eventually found themselves caught up in the conflict.

A humanitarian initiative, Lifeline's provision of relief proved a highly political act.   "Relief is not a value-free operation," observed RRC Commissioner Ibrahim Abu Ouf.   "It does not work in a vacuum.   It is based on the interests of the countries involved, whether the Sudan or others.   It has a cultural and a religious dimension.   It is a network of sometimes conflicting interests and forces pushing toward different goals, though dressed up in the same garb."

The Lifeline experience demonstrates that humanitarian imperatives exercise no automatic legitimacy or compelling authority
when political or military forces are otherwise inclined. Yet it
also suggests that humanitarian concerns, creatively managed,
can be an influential force in their own right. Even where
political and military agendas are dominant, humanitarian
concerns can make their mark.

The Sudan Government and the Insurgents

The most critical interaction between politics and relief involved
the decisions of the warring parties to allow the establishment
of Lifeline and to participate in it. The common perception is
that both sides embraced Lifeline at a time when, for political
and military reasons, it was advantageous for them to do so
-- and then extricated themselves when Lifeline no longer
served their interests. Many observers therefore conclude that
any "humanitarianism" by either side was opportunistic. At
least, they say, it failed when put to the test.

It is true that the protagonists endorsed Lifeline at a time when
it was clearly in their political and military interests to do so.
Appendix B traces the interplay of events during the years
immediately preceding Lifeline. By early 1989 the beleaguered Sudan army had suffered a string of major defeats
in the south. There was growing unrest in the north as well.
The government of Sadiq el Mahdi was weak and vulnerable.
The army and all political parties except the NIF were pressing
for an end to the war. Lifeline provided a reprieve on the
battlefield and a chance for the regime to regroup politically as
well.

If the government endorsed Lifeline out of weakness, the
insurgents did so more from a position of strength. Nonetheless, by early 1989 they too had reasons for welcoming a

reprieve. Rapid military successes had outrun their ability to govern the areas taken. They needed time to consolidate control, provide services to the civilian population, and cultivate its loyalty. SPLA forces, like their opposite numbers, also wanted to prepare for the next stage in the war. They could use a breather until the rains came and then determine whether to resume fighting, capitalizing at that point on their rainy season advantage over the Sudanese army, which was less mobile on the ground.

Yet however persuasive the military calculations, humanitarian considerations also played a significant role in each side's thinking. The center column in Appendix B identifies the humanitarian agenda that forced its way onto the political and military landscape.

As the cumulative human tragedy of the years 1983-88 became more widely known, international and domestic pressure to deal with the humanitarian emergency grew. Censured for retrograde economic and human rights policies, the government saw Lifeline as a way of reinstating itself with the international community and responding to increasingly vocal elements at home. The SPLA, whose attacks on relief convoys and civilian commercial aircraft had drawn particular censure, also stood to benefit from being seen to be more concerned about civilian lives.

Each party could thus gain from accepting help in meeting the needs of civilian populations that neither, realistically speaking, could address. Providing more effectively for civilian populations, whether in garrison towns or the countryside, would in turn have strategic value. For each side, this benefit outweighed the costs of allowing civilians to be assisted in areas that, in any event, were outside its direct control. Both welcomed resources at a time of financial austerity and, while accepting aid, would work to control its intrusiveness.

For each side, the decision to participate thus involved a careful weighing of costs and benefits. In fact, participation was part of a broader set of calculations using food as a political weapon, though each side disclaimed such a strategy. "If the government had used food as a political weapon," observed Abdul Hamid Latif, the Sudan's Ambassador to Kenya, in early 1990, "we would have barred food to the rebels." While he may be correct in a narrow sense, government policies such as the arming of tribal militias sought to disrupt food production and prevent people from meeting their own food needs. Ultimately, too, the government did seek to bar assistance by suspending relief flights into the south.

The insurgents, too, disclaimed the use of food as a political strategy. "We have not used food as a weapon," said SPLA commander Riak Macar in March 1990, "because we do not have it." Again, in a narrow sense, he was correct. However, in the years before Lifeline, SPLA strategy had been to prevent food from getting into areas controlled by the government. During Lifeline itself, the availability of relief was part of the SPLA's strategy of encouraging people to return home and of meeting the food needs of people affected by the fighting.

In agreeing to Lifeline, each side sought to assure that aid would serve its own needs. The Khartoum authorities looked to the RRC, the insurgents to the SRRA, to impose administrative and political controls on outside assistance. At the same time, each side sought to be identified positively with aid activities, though the insurgents had more to gain politically from association with aid programs than did the government. (See box, p. 83)

It is not clear to what extent political considerations also figured in specific allocations decisions by the authorities about which areas should receive aid. On various occasions, food was used to win the allegiance of local populations or to dampen unrest. Food helped the SPLA control the Toposa

Citizens in Juba, a government-held town largely cut off from the surrounding countryside, were kept alive by food flown in and distributed by private relief groups. Newly arrived families receive rations from the Red Cross in May 1989.
ICRC/T. Gassmann

tribe, for example, whose raids had disrupted the passage of relief convoys from Kenya into southeastern Equatoria. By and large, however, allocations appear to have reflected actual need. Certainly international aid officials insisted that civilian needs be respected in aid distribution.

The relief provided by Lifeline had demonstrable effects, economic and political alike. In government-controlled areas, the availability of food quickly broke the monopoly exercised by Arab merchants. Because it did so, some have speculated that merchants may have directed violence against relief operations. In SPLA-controlled areas, too, the effect of the arrival of food on local prices was immediate and its contribution to reviving languishing local economies substantial.

Relief also eased the need of political authorities themselves to provide food. This was particularly helpful to the government because civilian populations in garrison towns represented a political powder keg. The availability of large amounts of relief also spared the government the choice between committing scarce foreign exchange for food purchases and forcing civilians to tighten their belts further still. Civilians in SPLA-controlled areas, which tended to be rural, had a better chance of providing for their own food needs, though there, too, aid eased political discontent.

There was an equally complex interaction between relief and military matters. Because military authority prevailed in both government and SPLA-controlled areas, Lifeline officials had difficulty in assuring that only civilians received relief. Aid distributions everywhere, whether by the RRC and the SRRA or by outside aid agencies, required approval of the military and sometimes even its logistics support. One of the major obstacles delaying the relief train from Muglad to Aweil, for example, was the need for consent from the various local military officials responsible for the areas along its route. "Anyone who moves in our territory does so with our authority," observed Commander Riak Macar in explaining that SPLA presence made it possible for NGOs to deliver food.

Sometimes military personnel were very cooperative. In fact, sometimes they were more seized with relief needs than were civilian officials. Yet other times they were not. In one incident outside Malakal, the SPLA relieved civilians returning home of just-distributed relief food. Government army officials responded by allowing civilians to come to Malakal to receive food and consume it on the spot but not to carry any back to their villages. On one occasion in Wau, the Sudan army sent civilians to collect relief from aid officials on its behalf.

There were various skirmishes between aid officials and the military over the control of relief supplies. On one occasion the SPLA requested food for the guards at the Yirol airstrip but backed off when the ICRC explained that such food was intended only for civilian use. Aid officials on several occasions were denied access to relief warehouses and distribution records in circumstances that suggested improprieties by the military. One NGO closed a program in eastern Equatoria because of lack of cooperation from the local SPLA commander.

The challenge that faced the aid agencies of assuring that only civilians received relief food was complicated in SPLA areas by the fact that the insurgents used as soldiers boys as young as thirteen or fourteen years of age. In normal relief settings, male teenagers would be given relief assistance without question. Since most families had at least one member in the SPLA, food distributions among civilians clearly fortified some in the army as well. James Duku, Nairobi-based SRRA liaison officer, disputes reports that the SRRA gave relief food directly to the military. He acknowledges, however, that when civilians in an area qualified for relief food, their soldier-relatives also benefited.

How much relief food reached the military through one means or another is difficult to determine. There is no doubt that Lifeline experienced difficulty in preventing food from falling into military hands. "The men with the guns always eat first, or at least they always eat," observes Roger Winter of the US Committee for Refugees. "They're not going to starve, whether they are government soldiers in garrison towns or the SPLA." When military posts were overrun, relief food was sometimes found, although it is hard to establish whether more than a small fraction of Lifeline's total commodities were involved. It is widely believed that there were more such abuses by the SPLA than by government troops.

As aid agencies hurried to move food during the early months of Lifeline, there was probably more "leakage" than once an extensive network of food monitors had been established. Donor governments waived standard reporting requirements in the interests of speeding aid to those in need. Even when monitoring had improved and more rigorous requirements were in place, Lifeline's civil war setting posed a greater challenge than would a humanitarian emergency resulting from a natural disaster. The receipt of food by its intended beneficiaries could never be taken for granted.

The Siege of Juba

Juba was kept alive from late 1988 onward largely by NGOs. Private relief groups airlifted and distributed food donated by governments and UN agencies to a population of some 250,000 civilians. NGOs and the ICRC also helped meet health, water, agriculture, and training needs.

Juba's civilians were in double jeopardy. The city, which also housed the largest army unit in the south of some 20,000 soldiers, was encircled by army outposts designed to keep the SPLA out. Civilians seeking to leave were sometimes killed by government troops. Juba was also ringed by SPLA land mines that wounded some who tried to exit despite the risks. SPLA shells lobbed into the city killed or wounded others. The government claimed that civilians remained because the countryside was insecure; the SPLA, that people were hostages of the government. Both were true. Appeals to allow civilians safe passage from the beleaguered city were in vain.

In January 1990 the SPLA stepped up military pressure on Juba following the capture of nearby towns. UN buildings, a camp for displaced persons, the hospital, and an NGO project -- but no military installations -- were hit. UN officials and Western diplomats arranged the evacuation of international aid personnel. For twelve hours on January 29, the government suspended its flight ban and the SPLA agreed not to shoot at non-military aircraft. Two ICRC delegates remained; most other international aid personnel departed, returning in March or April when the military situation had eased.

Whether or not much food fell into military hands -- and most observers believe that the great bulk of it did not -- the availability of food to civilian populations had an important bearing on the war itself. "When you're at war," observes John Beavan, Britain's Ambassador to Khartoum, "everything becomes a question of military and strategic advantage." The ICRC confirms as much from its own experience. "If you get food to a beleaguered town," observes Andreas Lendorff, "it clearly goes against a military strategy. In some circumstances, whatever you do from a relief standpoint will have negative implications for military objectives."

From the government's perspective, the issue was not that of supplying beleaguered towns, which were in its own hands, but of permitting relief to the countryside. In some government circles, particularly among the military, recalls RRC Commissioner Abu Ouf, there was a "higher temperature" against aid activities because they were suspected of strengthening the insurgency. "An army can be defeated from the kitchen," he notes, "so military people quite naturally want to shut the kitchen door."

The interaction between relief and military considerations is illustrated by the situation of civilians in Juba. (See box, p. 72) The SPLA mined the road into Juba to prevent military supplies from entering, but keeping out food for civilians at the same time. The Sudan government authorities in Juba refused to provide military escorts for relief convoys into the town, and the UN would not have accepted them had they been offered. Private relief vehicles, having then attached themselves to convoys that included military goods, were attacked by the SPLA. While relief supplies may not have been the target of either side, they were clearly a casualty of the strategies adopted.

Lifeline's non-food activities were spared much of the attention its food component attracted. "People don't mind giving injections to kids," observes WFP Executive Director James Ingram, "but it's more difficult to keep food from getting to armies. Wars have always been about control of food supplies." Dividing vaccines and educational supplies between the protagonists also proved less contentious than dividing food aid. Moreover, non-food items were more readily limited to civilian beneficiaries.

The effects of participation in Lifeline also had military implications. Food provided to garrison towns, in addition to keeping civilian populations alive, helped maintain government control. On one occasion, the military commander in Juba, in danger of losing such control, used the threat of allowing civilians to leave the encircled city as a means of pressuring his Khartoum superiors to let them be resupplied with food. Food provided in SPLA areas improved the quality of life and increased stability and popular support for the SPLA.

Both sides benefited from the reprieve associated with Lifeline. They used the interlude to strengthen and consolidate their military positions and accused each other of doing so. Relief freed up resources to spend on preparing for and fighting the war. Reviewing the government's request from Lifeline for 1990, one observer notes that food provided from outside would ease the government's need to use locally produced grain to feed its own people. Outside food aid "would replace home-grown sorghum which the government has been exporting to get hold of desperately needed foreign exchange. That foreign currency is used to feed the war."[2]

Did either side derive disproportionate military or political benefit from Lifeline? On the military side of the ledger, each of the warring parties benefited but neither lost much. Some territory did change hands during Lifeline: the town of Bor fell to the SPLA in mid-April, as did portions of southern

Equatoria around Kajo Kaji and Yei in early 1990. The government also retook several areas. The connection to Lifeline, however, was remote.

By most accounts, Lifeline's benefits were more political than military. The Sudan's Ambassador to the US Abdalla Ahmed Abdalla believes that Lifeline benefited both sides about equally. He concedes, however, that Lifeline gave the insurgents a slight edge by virtue of their enhanced international stature. After all, he observes wryly, before Lifeline the Sudan government was already a government. That perception appears to have figured in Khartoum's imposition of tighter controls over Lifeline activities in 1990 and, conversely, in the insurgents' dissatisfaction with the new arrangements.

Did the resurgence of the war in late October reflect a waning commitment to humanitarian principle? As humanitarian need had not been controlling in the decision of either party to agree to Lifeline in the first place, neither was it a decisive deterrent to their resumption of fighting. The fact that political/military considerations eventually brought down the curtain on the tranquility enjoyed by Lifeline did not mean that humanitarian considerations were unimportant -- only that they were not overriding. In the involvement of both parties in Lifeline from start to finish, then, the interplay of humanitarian with other factors is clear.

Other Governments

Political as well as humanitarian concerns also played a role in the involvement of many other governments in relief activities in the Sudan. Most prominent in pressing for the creation of Lifeline were the so-called "donor" governments. Foremost among them was the US, from which many other governments have traditionally taken their cues in matters relating to humanitarian aid, refugees, and development.

The US had been the leading donor in the international response to the Sudan famine of 1984-85 and to the Sudan throughout the entire decade. The US alone provided more aid in 1984-85 than did Lifeline as a whole in 1989. US grant food aid over a twelve-month period during the earlier famine was 250,000 metric tons, more than double all food aid through Lifeline in 1989. The value of US aid to the Sudan in 1986 -- humanitarian, economic, and military combined -- reached $346 million, well above Lifeline's grand total three years later.

Predominantly geopolitical considerations made the Sudan the largest recipient of US aid in sub-Saharan Africa during the eighties. In fact, forceful public US criticism of Khartoum policies on humanitarian and human rights grounds was muted by US interest in continued base rights for its rapid deployment force and access to the Red Sea, strategic proximity to Marxist Ethiopia, investment opportunities for US oil companies, and support for the Sudan's ally Egypt and for the Sudan government itself, which alone among Arab governments had backed the Camp David Agreement on the Middle East. Late in the decade, humanitarian considerations received higher priority as lessened superpower tensions and the Mahdi government's cultivation of Libya altered political calculations.

State Department officials have a different view. Norman Anderson, US Ambassador in Khartoum from 1986-89, denies that humanitarian interests were ever given short shrift. Throughout this period, he recalls, US geopolitical interests in the Sudan were not substantial and the Sudan was "a very weak reed" to rely on. "Humanitarian considerations were much greater than military ones for the US," he says in 1990 of US policy toward the Sudan during the period since 1985.

The decisive push for Lifeline came not from high-level State Department officials in Khartoum or Washington but from the Office of Foreign Disaster Assistance (OFDA) within the State Department's US Agency for International Development (AID). Leading the charge was OFDA's energetic director Julia Taft, who saw the suffering in the Sudan primarily in moral terms. "I don't believe any nation has the right to starve its own people," she said.

During the latter half of 1988, she and her staff were seized with the need to find ways of assisting civilians throughout the Sudan. They sought to enlist everyone possible: Secretary of State George P. Shultz and senior US diplomats, other governments far and near, NGOs, and the UN itself. They helped UN officials put together what became the plan of action for the Khartoum conference, attended by Taft as the highest ranking Western aid official. OFDA's Sudan efforts, temporarily upstaged by Central American hurricane and Armenian earthquake late in 1988, bore fruit with the launching of Lifeline in early 1989.

One of the earliest signs of a shift in US policy came with a statement approved by the new Secretary of State James A. Baker, 3rd on January 23, 1989. In one of the Bush Administration's first foreign policy actions, the US announced its intention to provide aid to civilians in SPLA-controlled areas. State Department officials credit the change to the policy review stimulated by OFDA rather than to a fresh initiative by the new administration. For several months, NGOs in the US had worked hard to push the Administration and the Congress in that direction.

Also strongly supportive of a major humanitarian initiative in the Sudan was the Dutch government. Had the Dutch had their way, Lifeline would have been established well before the Americans began to press for it. Their response reflected three elements central to Dutch foreign policy, explains Martin Koper of the Netherlands Embassy in Nairobi: a priority to provide humanitarian assistance in armed conflicts, a concern for protecting human rights, and support for the work of NGOs.

The Dutch government was well informed about the deteriorating situation, thanks to information received through NGOs and to relationships established during decades of direct aid activities, activities halted in 1984 due to security considerations. Dutch aid averaged about $60 million annually, somewhat more in 1986-87 in support of progress toward democratization and somewhat less at the end of the decade to express concerns about human rights violations and economic policies. A greater portion of Dutch assistance to both sides was channeled through NGOs and the ICRC in 1988 and through them and Lifeline in 1989-90. Aid was "part of our dialogue with the Sudan government," says a Foreign Ministry official in the Hague. While such assistance "can't turn around the whole atmosphere," he concedes, it has proved a useful way of keeping communications open and conveying concerns.

"Humanitarian assistance, peace, and national reconciliation are Canada's assistance policies," explains Richard Chappell of the Ministry of External Affairs in Ottawa. Canadian aid to the Horn of Africa during the eighties totaled over $300 million, most of it directed toward emergency needs. That has occasioned a policy review to determine whether such assistance would not have been more effective had it addressed the underlying causes of what have now become protracted emergencies. Canada thus gave Lifeline its blessing and, like the Dutch, encouraged it to address the roots of the suffering.

The British government also played a major role in Sudan relief, reflecting historical ties, commercial interests, and humanitarian concerns. The United Kingdom (UK) provided almost one fifth of Lifeline's total resources in 1989, funding NGO activities such as those of Oxfam-UK as well as the work of UN agencies. The UK also played a leadership role among representatives of donor governments based in Khartoum, pressing the authorities particularly energetically to reinvigorate Lifeline in 1990. The government of Italy was also involved early on, donating sixty trucks in 1986 and foodstuffs in 1987 before supporting Lifeline itself in 1989-90.

A mixture of humanitarian and political considerations also figured in the heavy involvement of the EC in Lifeline. Well in advance of its launching, EC representatives in Khartoum and Nairobi were active behind-the-scenes supporters of NGO efforts to mount programs on both sides of the conflict. During Lifeline itself, the EC contributed substantial amounts of funding and food to UN agencies, Sudanese political authorities, the ICRC, and NGOs. The EC was content to let the UN take the lead, make the basic operational decisions, and provide the necessary monitoring. It did not seek much independent visibility for itself.

Given the importance humanitarian considerations had come to exercise in the thinking of donor governments, could a major relief effort have been mounted sooner? The fact that some 500,000 lives were lost during the years 1986-88 makes the question of more than passing interest. There is, indeed, some evidence to suggest an affirmative answer. Had the US and the EC been willing to play a more assertive role, comments Alex de Waal, a seasoned observer of the Sudan scene, "Lifeline could have happened in 1986."

Again, Ambassador Anderson disagrees. "We all knew from 1983 on that the civil war was creating various states of famine," he recalls. "The surprise was only the degree." He says he pressed Prime Minister el Mahdi on every possible occasion to let relief go to both sides. He believes representations were not more effective because of limited leverage due to US and other government cutbacks in economic and military aid. If the US soft-pedalled humanitarian concerns, he asserts, it was for humanitarian reasons: to avoid a backlash against US-supported *humanitarian* activities in the north.

The UN official who led the Lifeline negotiations agrees that it would have been difficult to mount Lifeline before 1989. "Politically the time was not ripe," recalls Under-Secretary-General Abdulrahim A. Farah a year later. In 1989, however, "When the warring parties realized the tragic impact of the drought and the tremendous loss of civilian life brought about by drought and war, they were willing to bury the hatchet -- or at least the sharp part of the hatchet."

But serious questions remain. The historical record tends to bear out the broad indictment, if not all the particulars, offered by one journalist in March 1989. The international community had been "negligent, complacent, unable or unwilling to act decisively in a manner that would have saved lives," wrote Raymond Bonner in *The New Yorker* magazine. "The United

Relief agency personnel discuss arrangements for displaced persons in Kapoeta, Southern Sudan.
International Rescue Committee/Jenny Sulgar

States, Britain, the Netherlands, France, Germany, Japan, the European Economic Community, the United Nations agencies said nothing." Bonner includes in his sweeping criticism NGOs, whose fear of expulsion, he says, tempered their outspokenness, and the media, which failed to "pursue the story as it had the famine in Ethiopia in 1984 and 1985."[3]

* * *

The only African country that played a major role in relief assistance to the Sudan was Kenya. It had urged aid activities since mid-1985 and well in advance of Lifeline had facilitated cross-border efforts from Kenya by private groups. "We told the Sudan's Ambassador about our concern and our intention to become involved," explains Bethuel A. Kiplagat, Permanent Secretary of the Kenyan Foreign Affairs Ministry in April 1990. "It was no secret." As for Lifeline itself, "We pushed Lifeline from here." President Daniel Arap Moi was, he says, the only African head of state to condemn the imposition of *sharia*.

Humanitarian concerns also converged with Kenya's political and economic interests. Kenya, like neighboring Uganda, was affected by Sudanese cattle rustlers, refugees, and air force raids. In addition, economic ties to the landlocked region controlled by the SPLA stood to benefit Kenya. Some in the Kenyan government also viewed the insurgents as an ally deserving the assistance of black African states against its Arab and Muslim adversaries.

At the regional level, the Organization of African Unity (OAU) was conspicuous by its absence. "We would have been involved if we had been asked," says Dr. M.T. Mapuranga, an Assistant Secretary-General. "It is a task of the OAU to provoke the conscience of the international community and to mobilize it in the cause of saving African lives, whatever the political considerations may be." Although the Sudan government may not have requested the OAU's help, UN officials sought and received an OAU letter of encouragement as Lifeline was getting underway.

African and other voices have shown growing impatience, however, with the OAU's waiting-to-be-asked attitude. There were signs at the meeting of the Council of Ministers in July 1990 that the OAU door is slowly opening to issues that have been knocking more loudly during the eighties. The council passed a resolution endorsed by heads of state which, while not mentioning Lifeline by name, affirmed the importance of its principles for the continent as a whole.

In addressing the council the previous February, Secretary-General Salim Salim had expressed his intention "to take more seriously and enhance the organization's role as an active partner in efforts to resolve inter-African disputes. "Perhaps the time has come," he observed, "to explore ways by which the OAU can be allowed to be more original and imaginative in tackling Africa's problems. I am convinced that we should take a fresh look into how our organization can play its roles, especially in the field of conflict prevention, management, and resolution."[4]

Arab countries were even more conspicuous by their distance from Lifeline, despite what UN officials describe as extraordinary attempts to enlist their involvement. Egypt, with strategic interests in the Sudan and political connections to one of its major parties, appears to have wanted to avoid getting embroiled in the politics of the war. While neither Egypt nor other Arab countries made cash contributions, they view their membership in the UN itself as making them partners in Lifeline activities.

Several Arab governments, including Egypt, Saudi Arabia, and Iraq, had assisted the displaced around Khartoum after the 1988 floods. In fact, they had responded then more speedily than had traditional Western donor governments, although their action did not attract the international media attention that generally accompanies Western humanitarian aid. While Arab governments did not provide special funding to Lifeline, private contributions from individuals in Arab countries were received by Sudanese Muslim NGOs. Arab government officials suggest a preference for helping quietly and, where possible, through private channels.

The Union of Soviet Socialist Republics (USSR) and the countries of Eastern Europe played virtually no role in Lifeline. Preoccupied with its own problems, the USSR expressed

---

Civilians under Siege

Both the government and the insurgents adopted military and political strategies that violated the humanitarian and human rights of Sudanese civilians.

The SPLA appears to have worked harder to avoid abuses and to see that human needs were met. An insurgent movement dependent for material and moral support on the local population, the SPLM/A could ill afford to antagonize civilians unduly. SPLA policy requires severe punishment of renegade soldiers for actions such as robbery and rape. SPLA military policies caused serious hardship among civilians and on occasion the SPLA restricted aid agency access to them, citing security considerations.

The government has not appeared intent on winning the allegiance of the citizenry in areas it has controlled. Viewing civilians in towns such as Juba, Wau, and Malakal as "rebel sympathizers" who were perhaps on their way to becoming "rebels" themselves, the government was on occasion willing to interdict relief shipments to them. Yet it, too, has had an interest in avoiding the kind of widespread civilian discontent that could make governance more difficult.

interest but did not follow through. An early offer by Soviet diplomats to provide transport for relief supplies did not materialize because the Soviet Foreign Ministry lacked the hard currency needed to reimburse Aeroflot.

The Soviets, who at the time were applying heavy diplomatic and economic pressure on the Mengistu regime toward a negotiated settlement to the Ethiopian conflict, did not do the same in the Sudan, where they had substantial commercial and arms interests. Apart from membership in the UN itself, the countries of Eastern Europe did not participate in Lifeline, as they and the USSR had done in the 1984-85 Ethiopian famine relief effort.

In short, a mixture of humanitarian and political interests affected the priority and timing of the involvement of governments, individually and collectively, in relief activities in the Sudan. Had humanitarian considerations been more of a priority, joint action might have taken shape earlier. Governments eventually responded, however, led by the traditional donors and on a generally substantial scale.

Non-Governmental Organizations

The interplay of relief and politics seems a less likely subject for NGOs. However, political considerations figured in the motivations of a few NGOs and influenced the operations of others. NGOs were also influenced by institutional politics of their own. The results of their humanitarian activities had political consequences.

NGOs chose to work in the Sudan for a number of reasons. Some, like Norwegian People's Aid, have avowedly political purposes. "We are the relief organization of the Federation of

Trade Unions and the Social Democratic Party in Norway," explains NPA's Sudan representative Egil Hagen. NPA has a tradition of helping the underdogs and endorsing their causes, whether the republicans in the Spanish Civil War, the Tamils in Sri Lanka, the Palestinians in the Middle East, or the Eritreans and Tigrayans in the Horn. "Relief in war situations *is* politics," Hagen says. "I am one hundred percent with the SPLA. I don't make public statements to that effect but I do the maximum to see that they get the material aid they need, apart from weapons."

Other NGOs such as World Vision International disavow any influence of politics on their work. Their decision to assist people in SPLA-controlled areas and, before their expulsion, in government-controlled areas, they say, was simply a matter of helping where they were welcome. In their view, the substantial resources they receive from the US government for work in the Sudan do not compromise World Vision's neutrality, nor does their choice of NPA and the SRRA as operating partners. World Vision sees itself functioning in a political vacuum. "Politics don't affect us," states Leo Ballard, Associate Director of its East Africa Relief Operations. "I realize there are politics all around you, but you still have to focus on helping hungry people."

Most NGOs fall somewhere between the politicized humanitarianism of NPA and the purportedly apolitical approach of World Vision. They seek to chart a course that does not choose up sides yet acknowledges that humanitarian activities are circumscribed by political realities and have unavoidable political repercussions. Most NGOs sense that however nongovernmental their organizations, their activities are carried out in space provided by political authorities and subject to political abuse.

Most of the international NGOs with offices in Khartoum or Nairobi -- there are several dozen in each place -- would prefer as a matter of principle to work on both sides of the conflict. Such a geographical presence would convey an even-handedness that, as a practical matter, few agencies have managed to attain. Those with programs on both sides face a kind of double jeopardy. They are subject to political pressures from each protagonist and to being whipsawed between the two.

National Sudanese NGOs have also found it difficult to mount programs in SPLA-controlled areas while maintaining good

---

Private Agencies under Siege

Médecins sans Frontières (Doctors without Borders) has worked in the Sudan for more than a decade.

MSF-France began in northern Sudan in 1979 and in government and SPLA-controlled areas of the south in 1986. During 1986-88 it sought to alert the UN, governments, and the media to the ravages of the war and famine. In December, 1989 a duly marked MSF aircraft was shot down over Aweil in circumstances that pointed toward government responsibility. The pilot, two MSF staff, and a WFP consultant were killed. In protest, MSF-France withdrew its seventy expatriates, a serious setback to health services in the Sudan.

The following February, two **MSF-Belgium** staff persons were kidnapped from government-controlled Malakal. The action was taken by the local SPLA commander to demonstrate the SPLA's ability to operate with impunity in government-claimed areas. MSF-Belgium, already poised to leave following the December incident, closed its Sudan operations shortly thereafter. The aid personnel were returned unharmed.

MSF-Holland continues activities in the Sudan begun in 1984, believing that the urgent human needs and humanitarian principles are at stake which require its presence.

relations with the Sudan government. Organizations such as the SCC and Sudanaid whose constituencies span the civil war divide have apparently been discouraged from functioning in areas outside government control. The SPLM/A has agreed to allow NGOs that assist on the government side to work in insurgent areas but has been reluctant to welcome individual aid personnel who themselves have done so.

Most NGOs, therefore, work on either one side or the other, where they are confronted by "only" a single set of political pressures. "In modern wars," observes NPA's Hagen, "you don't have the luxury of establishing trust on both sides. NGOs choose one side and do the best they can." Whether the side be that of the government or the insurgency, NGOs have had to struggle to protect the humanitarian space within which to function. Like all other aid entities, including the RRC and the SRRA themselves, they have had to make shrewd judgments about when to press the authorities on matters of humanitarian principle and when simply to make the best of a bad situation. Their experience has corroborated the view, expressed about NGO activities worldwide, that "There are always powerful forces at work that want to make impartial organizations partial."⁵

Some NGOs also see their work as strengthening, in a broad sense, the hand of the political authorities in question. In fact, acknowledges one NGO executive, that is "part of the deal." He notes that "The very fact that we have decided to work in SPLA-controlled areas is a political statement." That is, his NGO has made the determination that in those areas conditions are such that it can provide humanitarian assistance with integrity. Some NGOs also agree with him that if hungry people truly benefit from outside assistance, their improved situation should and will affect the political landscape as well.

* * *

In the Sudan, where religious differences are one element in the civil war, the involvement of religious NGOs, Christian and Muslim alike, has political implications. Religious groups approach their humanitarian mission from a variety of perspectives. Some view providing aid as an end in itself, a genuine but disinterested expression of religious commitment. Others see it as a more explicit statement of faith and an overt invitation to others to embrace their viewpoint. Most agencies make available aid to people irrespective of the religion of the recipient. Many are committed to strengthening local religious institutions   to carry out   a range of community -- and religious -- activities.

One religious NGO frames its purpose in SPLA areas as that of identifying with the oppressed, regardless of their tribal, ethnic, political, or religious affiliations.   Yet its activities are carried out through Sudanese religious institutions and include support for pastors, their families, and their pastoral work. At the same time, the NGO's director indicates, "If the government of the Sudan invited us to work in a Muslim community, we would give the invitation serious consideration."

Khartoum authorities have grave misgivings about activities they view as essentially religious and political, humanitarian elements notwithstanding. In fact, they see Lifeline itself, and not just religious NGOs, as an expression of the religious and political agenda of the Christian West.   The circumstantial evidence is compelling: Western nations with predominantly Christian populations are channeling funds through Christian NGOs to churches engaged in religious activities in areas in rebellion against a Muslim government.

RRC Commissioner Abu Ouf welcomes humanitarian assistance devoid of hidden agendas. In fact, he views the sacredness of the person as part of the common religious property of humankind. "If you take a committed Muslim, a committed Christian, a committed Jew, a committed Hindu, each is committed to the welfare of the larger community." On the other hand, he says, if NGOs through their relief activities "want to shape, redirect, influence my belief as a Muslim, they are not my cup of tea." In this context, the government's preference for Muslim NGOs is understandable.

The SPLM is more comfortable with the presence and involvement of Christian NGOs. It acknowledges the spiritual needs of people in its areas. In fact, a number of its commanders have taken a personal interest in rebuilding church structures and in promoting church-related activities. The SPLM/A has also sought to enlist the churches and receive their blessing on its cause. Welcoming the space provided in which to function, church leaders at the same time have sought to preserve a certain distance between their own activities and the insurgent movement.

* * *

Although caught up in the political crosscurrents of the civil war, NGOs did not become a very effective political force in their own right within the Sudan. Given the heterogeneity of NGOs and the fundamental differences of understandings of politics and the political, a "common front" would have been surprising had it developed. "In any situation, there will be diversity of opinions within the NGO community," remarks Johan Balslev, who directs LWF's emergencies program from Geneva. "That's part of life." However, the absence of a cohesive community in either Khartoum or Nairobi has limited NGO ability to respond to challenges and protect humanitarian space from intrusion.

NGOs of course established day-to-day working relationships with each other in both places. In Khartoum, the Sudan Council of Voluntary Agencies (SCOVA) played a role, although somewhat limited, in stimulating dialogue among

NGOs, both national and expatriate. In Nairobi, NGOs met regularly to exchange information and views. But in both locations community-wide discussions seldom led to joint action. The Nairobi sessions were even chaired by UN officials and, preoccupied with Lifeline matters, did not address the full range of NGO concerns or plan common NGO strategies.

On occasion, effective cooperation demonstrated the value of joint action. In 1988 eight agencies associated with CART faced a crisis when ten new relief trucks were commandeered by the Sudan army in Juba for its military operations. The agencies lobbied together to win the release of the trucks and to prevent the loss of additional vehicles. "The public profile of the joint operation," an observer noted, "helped in making clear to the SPLA that the trucks while commandeered were not on CART business, and when they were returned that they were not still on army business."[6]

For the most part, however, NGOs did not function as a community bound together by common purposes and proceeding according to agreed upon ground rules. Most NGOs saw themselves as agencies with operational tasks to perform, not as organizations embodying a set of fundamental humanitarian principles. Many agencies seemed unable to look beneath the frictions they experienced with Lifeline to its underlying principles, which they at least implicitly shared.

As a result, NGOs were unable to deal effectively with direct challenges to their integrity. When the government charged first Lifeline and then its associated agencies with having transported military supplies and personnel, no concerted NGO response was forthcoming or even possible. Yet the government's allegations, however frivolous in appearance, were still grave and were used to curtail humanitarian operations for almost half a year. An NGO initiative to state NGO principles and set up a mechanism to encourage their observance might have made it easier to rebuff government charges. Joint action might also have preempted the UN's circulation of a Letter of Association with Lifeline described in the following chapter. Nor did NGOs harness the power represented by their delivery of relief to extract greater respect from the authorities on either side.

Heterogeneity among NGOs has traditionally been an obstacle to joint action, particularly in the area of the development of codes of professional conduct. The situation in the Sudan confirmed the general observation that "Some organizations operating in the humanitarian sphere appear to have no formal or binding guiding principles which could be said to be of a humanitarian nature, while others appear to subscribe to a variety of more or less fixed or flexible objectives falling broadly within a general humanitarian concept."[7] The pressures of functioning in the Sudan doubtless accentuated such differences while at the same time underscoring the need for greater commonality of purpose. In other highly politicized

Two displaced Dinka workers prepare a Red Cross/Red Crescent warehouse for the rains.
UNICEF/Mariantonietta Peru

situations such as relief operations with Afghan refugees in Pakistan, a common front was established among an even larger field of NGOs.

* * *

Relief and politics also converged in the education and advocacy activities of NGOs. Both warring parties rightly viewed NGOs not just as relief agencies but as influential links to governments, the UN, the media, and the international public. They therefore sought to enlist NGOs as proponents of their respective causes. But NGO activities in these matters cut both ways. In addition to advocating more assistance to the Sudan, NGOs made known their frequently highly critical views of the war and the warring parties themselves.

The government expected praise for its decision to cooperate with Lifeline. Instead, General Bashir complains, the Sudan was pilloried for its human rights record. The insurgents, too, were nettled when NGOs insisted on greater fidelity by the SPLA to the rights and needs of civilian populations. Two incidents which illustrate the international political involvement of NGOs suggest they may have been more effective as advocates outside the Sudan than within.

First, Canadian NGOs in 1989-90 were exploring ways to play a more active role in the Sudan. Following a study of the Sudan crisis, the Canadian Council for International Co-operation adopted a resolution criticizing recent actions taken by the Khartoum authorities. It expressed the view that "Canadian bilateral financial support allows the government of Sudan to use other funds for the perpetuation of the war effort and the costs of suppressing its own population." NGOs urged the Canadian government to "withdraw all bilateral assistance . . . and redirect finances as appropriate, to the humanitarian and development programs of Sudanese and Canadian non-governmental organizations working in the Sudan."[18]

Second, Chairman John Garang in mid-1989 undertook an extended tour of foreign capitals seeking financial and political support for the SPLM cause. After a year of military victories and several months of cooperation with Lifeline, he seemed to expect warm welcomes as the conquering hero. He was well received as he articulated with eloquence the Movement's vision of a New Sudan.

In both Europe and the US, however, Garang faced tough questioning by NGOs about the tragic human effects of SPLA policies. In Washington, NGOs expressed particular alarm about the plight of civilians in Juba. "If I can take Juba, I will take Juba," Garang countered. At the same time, he acknowledged, "It is necessary to have humanitarian considerations in mind at all times and in all circumstances."

Pressed by NGOs on the SPLA's commitment to observe the international laws of war, Garang conceded that "We don't even have a copy of the Geneva Conventions." Yet he expressed his firm intention that the SPLA respect the Geneva Conventions and Protocols, for example, in its treatment of captured prisoners. He also offered to make his officers available to the ICRC for its standard training course, provided the Red Cross would seek them out and conduct its courses in the field.

With respect both to NGOs and to the politics of humanitarian assistance, the ICRC is in a category by itself. (See box, p. 135) The ICRC seeks to differentiate itself from NGOs, governments, and UN agencies, whose activities it applauds but whose approaches it sometimes finds lacking in important qualities of humanitarian assistance. While the ICRC saw its own activities as contributing to Lifeline's goals, it went to great lengths to preserve its own identity. The fact that the ICRC itself was badly buffeted by political crosscurrents confirms the complex connections between relief and politics in the Sudan.

The United Nations

Finally, the interplay between politics and relief affected the involvement of the UN. In the late eighties the UN had gained new stature as a result of diplomatic breakthroughs and peacekeeping operations in Afghanistan, Iran-Iraq, Angola, Namibia, and Central America. Yet it had found conflicts in the Horn of Africa far more intractable.

Excluded from a role in the Ethiopian civil war by the Mengistu regime and unsuccessful in assisting amid Somalia's civil strife, the Sudan seemed a more promising arena. In the years preceding Lifeline, however, the UN had failed, despite mounting evidence of extreme need, to make either a substantial diplomatic or humanitarian contribution. Efforts of dedicated international civil servants to reach people in the south had been rebuffed. (See box, p. 109)

In addition to the UN's own interest in making its mark, it offered a convenient vehicle for governments, themselves largely excluded from assisting in the south, to become involved without accepting the diplomatic consequences for their intervention. Governments that were themselves having great difficulty getting the attention of the Khartoum authorities were quite willing to see the UN shoulder the lead responsibility. The EC and the OAU were themselves comfortable with the UN playing that role as well.

The nature of the UN as an intergovernmental body influenced its involvement in relief. Constituted of member states, the UN represented the interests, political and humanitarian alike, of governments. Some insurgent movements -- the Palestine Liberation Organization and South West Africa People's Organization before Namibian independence -- enjoyed UN observer status, but the SPLM was not among them.

شريان الحياة
Life-Line

A cartoon depicting world response to the southern Sudan appeared in the Khartoum newspaper *Al-Watan* in early May 1989.

As indicated earlier, Lifeline reflected the UN's structural bias toward governments. It was negotiated principally with the Sudan government and finalized at a meeting of governments in the Sudan's capital. Despite Lifeline's links to the Khartoum authorities, however, the SPLM/A recognized it as a serious attempt to deal with human needs in SPLA-held areas. When sought out by UN officials once the government was on board, the insurgents agreed to the Khartoum plan of action with only minor changes.

Over time, however, the perception of the UN's role as honest broker between competing political authorities suffered. The shift on October 1, 1989 from Grant to Priestley and from New York to Khartoum cost Lifeline hard-won credibility with the SPLA. The changes appeared to downgrade the profile of the operation and to lodge its management firmly in "enemy territory." The UN's even-handedness was further called into question by the Lifeline 2 Agreement in March 1990, which reasserted the principle of assistance to civilians on both sides but gave the government relatively more monitoring authority.

The proposed food allocations also reflected concessions made in order to win government agreement to Lifeline 2. After having received 24 percent of the food in Lifeline 1, the insurgents were assured of only 15 percent of the food in Lifeline 2. While the allocation included a reserve of 12 percent which would be open to either side, the SPLM/A assumed that the reserve, too, would go disproportionately to the government. Even had it not, the SPLM/A believed the new allocations did not accommodate needs in insurgent areas, areas which had themselves expanded since March 1989.

The Suspension of Relief Flights

Following the October 1989 bombing of the SPLA-held town of Yirol, the government closed Sudan airspace to all relief flights pending an investigation. Many believe that the bombing itself was a pretext for suspending relief activities, a hypothesis strengthened by the fact that the government never issued a report on the investigation it promised to carry out.

The flight ban imposed a few days later in November applied initially to all relief flights -- even those into areas not controlled by the Sudan government. However, an exception was later made for government-controlled Juba when food shortages caused widespread discontent. The ban also did not apply to aircraft with commercial and military cargo bound for government-held destinations. Defying the ban and outraging the government, some NGOs continued relief flights from Kenya into non-government controlled areas.

Until lifted in April following agreement on Lifeline 2, the ban crippled many relief operations, though some relief supplies continued to be transported overland. Aircraft were critical to the movement of aid personnel and of perishable items such as vaccines to the more remote destinations.

During the initial Lifeline phase, Chairman Garang observed in May 1990, "the ice was broken, which made it possible for relief supplies to reach the people who needed them on both sides. Now there is not the same understanding and cooperation over relief." The UN's failure to treat the SPLM/A as a full partner became a more serious political liability in Lifeline 2, with potentially major consequences for the future.

Lifeline's bias toward the political interests of sovereign states also affected the UN's working relationships with NGOs. A number of NGOs, especially those working in SPLA-controlled areas, expressed appreciation that Lifeline had protected and expanded the humanitarian space in which they operated. They credited the UN umbrella with improving security and enhancing the movement of expatriate personnel in the south. The UN won agreement for NGOs to be allowed to have radios and occasionally dissuaded the authorities from expelling individual NGO staff persons who were no longer welcome. UN-negotiated exchange rates stretched the value of aid agency resources from 4.5 to 12.2 Sudanese pounds per US dollar.

At the same time, the added visibility that Lifeline has given to NGOs made them more subject to scrutiny and pressure. The Khartoum authorities came to view them as not closely enough tied to Lifeline, the insurgents as too closely connected. Thus in 1990 the government insisted that the UN increase its monitoring and coordination role over NGOs, the SPLM/A that governments fund NGOs directly and without any relation to Lifeline.

As indicated in the previous chapter, the involvement of various individual UN agencies, loosely coordinated under the Lifeline umbrella but each with its own institutional terms of reference and politics, also affected the implementation of relief activities.

* * *

In sum, Lifeline reflected a complex amalgam of humanitarian and political factors. In agreeing to participate in it, the warring parties had political as well as humanitarian objectives in mind. Other involved governments and aid agencies also had a blend of interests. While political and military objectives motivated the warring parties, humanitarian concerns also figured in their calculations. And although humanitarian aims animated the international community that mounted Lifeline, political factors affected the timing and execution of the relief program.

It is tempting to focus on the interaction between relief and politics at the level of individual commanders and civilian officials, politicians and aid personnel, the government and the insurgents. In that theater, humanitarian interests won some of the skirmishes and lost others. In a grander sense, however, Lifeline was an effort to counter the negative use of food as a political weapon through the deployment of relief and those providing it as a force for protecting and sustaining life. That larger contest, at mid-1990, is ongoing and still unresolved.

Chapter 4
Sovereignty and Suffering

The solution to the tension between sovereignty and humanitarian concern lies in redefining the sovereignty issue. Within the sovereignty of states, all these humanitarian concerns can be addressed.

Dr. Gazuli D'Faallah
Former Prime Minister of the Sudan

Lifeline emphasized both sovereignty's prerogatives and its positive humanitarian content. It dealt with sovereignty issues without challenging the fundamental authority of states. A humanitarian intervention, Lifeline required and received approval and reinforcing action from both warring parties. Through creative humanitarian diplomacy, it persuaded the protagonists to fulfill their humanitarian obligations by drawing on the resources of the international community to relieve civilian suffering. Lifeline also worked to limit the invocation of sovereignty to block humanitarian activities.

Always a factor with which aid programs must reckon, sovereignty can be an even more critical constraint when civil war challenges a nation's identity and political authority. Unless humanitarian interests can find ways of coming to terms with sovereignty, relief efforts in such circumstances may well be frustrated. Lifeline demonstrated that with the consent of the warring parties, concerted international humanitarian action is possible even during a civil war. It is less instructive about how to proceed in the absence of such consent.

It is useful to trace the interplay between sovereignty and the relief of suffering from the standpoint not of political theory but of the actions of the warring parties and the aid agencies.

A look at how considerations of sovereignty affected the behavior of the protagonists is followed by an examination of the impact of sovereignty on the functioning of UN agencies, NGOs, and governments.

Sovereignty and the Protagonists

During the years immediately preceding Lifeline when an estimated 500,000 persons died from famine and civil strife, the Sudan government invoked its authority as sovereign power to *prevent* the alleviation of suffering in the south. It pressured relief agencies not to mount activities in SPLA-controlled areas and expelled those ignoring official directives.

The government succeeded during those years in keeping relief activities to a bare minimum. It was willing to forego assistance from agencies such as the ICRC, which insisted on helping people on both sides, in order to prevent relief from reaching people in areas it did not control. Faced with the invocation of sovereignty to block efforts to deal with a worsening emergency, the UN combined appeals to reason with the resourceful application of political persuasion to obtain agreement to mount a major relief effort spanning both sides.

Talking tough, James Grant guided each side through a trenchant article by Raymond Bonner entitled "Famine" in the March 1989 issue of *The New Yorker*. "Both sides in the war have deployed a silent weapon to kill women and children," Bonner had written of the use of food in the Sudan. "It is as much a part of their warfare as automatic rifles and land mines."[1] "This is the way the world looks at you in the Sudan," Grant recalls telling officials on both sides. He also remembers pointing out that Bonner was equally scathing of the UN for its inaction. Lifeline offered the protagonists -- and the UN itself -- a second chance.

Reflecting a year later on the UN's success in breaking the political impasse, the Sudan's former Minister of State for Foreign Affairs Francis M. Deng noted that "The suffering of people in the Sudan was a tremendous human tragedy which called for the bending of the rules of international relations, regardless of what the Sudanese government felt." A prominent member of a distinguished family from an area in northern Bahr el Ghazal that had borne the brunt of the 1988 tragedy, Deng observes that "The government, rather than being humiliated internationally by refusing to receive assistance, decided to take the lead, claim the moral high ground, and request international aid."

In making the best of a bad situation, the government was not acting with total cynicism. Sadiq el Mahdi, who gave Lifeline the necessary go-ahead, "was not an opportunist," recalls one of the Prime Minister's intimates. "He genuinely felt that Lifeline was a right for the victims of the war. He did not consider it his prerogative to deny assistance to them." The fact that the Prime Minister made the decision to cooperate in Lifeline reluctantly, perhaps even expecting that the SPLM/A would not go along, does not decrease its importance.

In agreeing to Lifeline, the government went to great lengths to make clear that it was doing so as an exercise of its sovereignty. In fact, Khartoum authorities explicitly stated that they were entrusting a portion of Sudan's sovereignty to the UN. "We have, in effect, conceded sovereignty over a large part of our territory to the United Nations," said Dr. Ohag Mohamed Musa, Minister of Social Welfare, Zaakat, and Relief, as Lifeline was launched. "We expect close monitoring by the United Nations."

How significant was the government's decision? In a pragmatic sense, Khartoum simply accepted the hard reality that it had little authority over areas to which relief would now be regularly provided. The government's decision recalls the

Emancipation Proclamation issued by US President Abraham Lincoln in 1862 at a low-point in the military fortunes of the Union in its war against the breakaway South.

Lincoln freed the slaves only in states in rebellion against central government authority -- that is, only in areas where he lacked power to enforce his decision. Regarded at the time as more symbolic than real, Lincoln's edict nonetheless transformed the war to preserve the Union into a war to abolish slavery. It was followed after the war by a constitutional amendment that did away with slavery throughout the nation. By contrast, the importance of el Mahdi's decision, widely heralded when announced, has faded from view.

Even with fortunes sagging, the Prime Minister's endorsement of Lifeline had pivotal significance. After all, the government could have continued to invoke its sovereignty to keep frustrating international aid efforts. The government's claims were not entirely a legal fiction and its agreement involved major concessions even in the areas it still controlled. Its cooperation opened the way for what would become a major relief initiative throughout the south, irrespective of who claimed control. Territory largely off limits to international personnel during the civil war now became generally accessible.

As the internationally recognized sovereign power, the government stood to lose more from agreeing to Lifeline than did the SPLM/A, which made no claims to sovereignty even over the areas it controlled. Firmly committed to "One Sudan," the insurgents had never questioned the government's sovereignty or sought to create a separate nation over which to rule. However, as de facto government in many areas, they, too, exercised the equivalent of sovereign rights in agreeing to Lifeline.

Once agreed to by both parties, Lifeline functioned as a vehicle through which the international community exercised a certain discipline on each side. The effects were remarkable for rather different reasons. While the Sudan was a party to the Geneva Conventions and Protocols, efforts had been unsuccessful at bringing government practice into line with international humanitarian law. Leverage was limited by aid cutbacks and the

---

Rhetoric and Reality

Many governments seem to take a rather relaxed view regarding compliance with humanitarian norms, as if by ratifying the [Geneva] Conventions they had been freed from all other obligations ... But as soon as they are directly or indirectly involved in an armed conflict, most States qualify, interpret or simply ignore the rules of humanity, evoking state interests and sovereign prerogatives. Political considerations prevail over humanitarian requirements and humanitarian concerns are used to further political aims.[3]

Independent Commission on International Humanitarian Issues

---

government's relative isolation within the international community. Yet particularly in 1989 Lifeline provided a means for assuring fuller accountability by the Sudan government to internationally recognized codes of conduct.

The discipline imposed on the insurgents was even more remarkable. As indicated earlier, the SPLM/A, though of course not a party to the Geneva Conventions and Protocols, had publicly expressed a willingness to function within their strictures. While the insurgents' fidelity to those standards was far from uniform, the Lifeline experience suggests that international aid can and should provide a means for holding insurgents, no less than governments, to internationally agreed upon standards of behavior.

"If insurgent movements expect to be dealt with in the same way as governments when it comes to humanitarian assistance," observes Barbara Hendrie, a close student of aid activities in the Horn, "then they must also expect to be bound by international law regarding the treatment of civilians." Since today's insurgents are sometimes tomorrow's governments, their cooperation in matters humanitarian can be an important point of entry into acceptance of international obligations more generally.

In actual practice, the limitations accepted by the government and the insurgents in embracing Lifeline were never absolute or unambiguous. The authority they exercised to provide humanitarian access could also be invoked to deny it. "We're always testing the concept of sovereignty," commented a senior UN official after a year of managing Lifeline, "and being tested." After all, he noted, "If the government has loaned us its sovereignty, it may always reclaim it."

In fact, before the ink was dry on the Khartoum plan of action, the agreement was targeted by the NIF as a violation of Sudanese national sovereignty. Having just left the ruling coalition in protest against policies it deemed "soft" on the non-Muslim south, the NIF expressed its views in strong terms on an issue of utmost political sensitivity. Lifeline was pictured as a foreign assault on the Sudan's national sovereignty, character, and interests, a dagger thrust at the Sudan's heart. The opposite view was portrayed by a cartoon in a Khartoum newspaper depicting the international community as a heart pumping life through Lifeline into the south. (See p. 95)

Disarray within the government bureaucracy added opportunities for delay to the already difficult task of implementing Lifeline. The RRC, focal point for delivering on the government's commitments, soon became a target of suspicion and intrigue. The Khartoum plan of action committed the government to provide access for relief personnel to civilians, but travel permits were required and, for additional aid personnel entering the country, visas. The lateness of the hour required transporting relief by air, but flights needed clearance. Some delays were understandable, but recurrent holdups suggested a rear-guard action to recapture lost sovereignty.

On the SPLM/A side as well, agreement to the plan of action did not mean instant implementation. The insurgents, too, wanted to keep controls on relief operations. On occasion they too denied the access promised to civilian populations. SPLA officials were no more relaxed than their adversary about having expatriates, equipped with vehicles and radios, on the loose in the south and in direct contact with the outside world. The SPLM/A decision to bar relief personnel whose passports had been stamped by Khartoum authorities injected "sovereign-esque" considerations, to say nothing of serious constraints, into relief activities.

Despite such difficulties, the early delays experienced by Lifeline, however serious, were manageable. Even after a military coup replaced the el Mahdi government with a regime in which Muslim fundamentalists held greater sway, Lifeline for a time succeeded in protecting the space within which aid could be provided.

Following the political and military complications described earlier, however, the Bashir regime moved in November 1989 to reassert some of the sovereignty el Mahdi was perceived to have ceded. The government finally agreed in March 1990 to extend Lifeline, but only after assuring itself of firmer control of relief activities. Asked about the delay, Bashir explained that "the sovereignty of the country" had been violated by abuses associated with Lifeline. He singled out "certain NGOs which, under the umbrella of Lifeline, started to transport war materials to the rebel movement." He stressed his intention to assure that "anything entering the Sudan should be relief assistance and nothing else."

UN officials who negotiated the new agreement confirm the government's intent. "The problems we faced with the formulation of Lifeline 2," explained Michael Priestley in April 1990, "reflected the deeply held belief by the new military government that too much national sovereignty had been conceded under Lifeline 1. Whilst the principles of Lifeline 1 and its enduring value as a precedent have finally, and somewhat grudgingly, been acknowledged by the government of the Sudan, we have been subject to heavy pressures to impose greater restrictions and controls over relief goods reaching SPLA-held areas."

Conversely, the SPLM/A resisted acceptance of any backsliding on the part of the Khartoum authorities. "From the SPLA side," explained Priestley, "there was a marked reluctance to accept any erosion of the political and other gains they achieved under Lifeline 1, and they remain very uncomfortable with the enhanced degree of monitoring and control sought by both the government of the Sudan and the donor community."

In retrospect, it is clear that both warring parties exercised their political authority to provide humanitarian space for Lifeline activities. Even if that space narrowed under the Bashir government, the continuation of Lifeline for a second year seems to represent a constructive use of the authority of each protagonist and an accomplishment for the UN as well.

Sovereignty and the United Nations

Considerations of sovereignty exercised a major constraint on the effectiveness of the UN system in responding to the humanitarian crisis in the Sudan. Chapter 1 reviewed some of the difficulties experienced by the UN in the years before Lifeline, Chapter 2 the nature of the UN's response in the form of Lifeline, and Chapter 3 some of the political deterrents to more effective action. With some feet on the accelerator, other feet on the brake, and many hands on the steering wheel, it is no wonder that the UN vehicle did not proceed on a more even course.

"The concept of the sovereignty of states prevents the UN from intervening in their internal affairs without the consent of the recognized government," observes F.T. Liu, who has advised each UN Secretary-General since the founding of the UN on dealing with humanitarian needs in situations of political turmoil. "On the other hand, the organization is committed to upholding human rights and humanitarian principles and cannot remain indifferent to the plight of the civilian population affected by the civil war."

The Secretary-General cannot proceed without the permission of the sovereign state in question. However, he may indeed respond to a request for assistance. That was what he did when he received an appeal from the Sudan government in late 1988. The UN was then faced with designing an initiative which elicited the consent of the insurgents without implying formal recognition of them.

Within the UN family of specialized agencies, only UNICEF has a recognized mandate to assist in civil war settings. That mandate is largely de facto, based on involvement in such civil wars as China (1946-47), Nigeria/Biafra, and, more recently, Mozambique, Angola, Uganda, Afghanistan, Cambodia, Sri Lanka, Lebanon, and el Salvador. In each, UNICEF has provided humanitarian assistance to civilians without conveying diplomatic recognition of the insurgency. In selecting UNICEF's chief to head Lifeline, the Secretary-General availed himself of UNICEF's recognized competence in such settings.

The situation in which only one UN agency has a mandate to be involved in such circumstances, however, is anomalous. "It's not enough for UNICEF to have the mandate," says James C. Ingram, WFP Executive Director. "WFP needs such a mandate too. There's hardly any political emergency that involves mass movements of people that will not invariably require large amounts of food."

WFP must await an invitation by the Secretary-General or by the recognized government before providing assistance. "We feel that it ought to be possible for a UN intergovernmental humanitarian organization to act in support of people who are suffering in areas beyond the control of the state in question," continues Ingram. "We can't really do that now."

The Sudan experience also indicates that once the UN has been invited to become involved, establishing and maintaining an impartial course is not easy. Under-Secretary-General for Special Political Questions Abdulrahim A. Farah, who laid the diplomatic groundwork for Lifeline, believes that despite the difficulties, the UN acquitted itself well. "The UN has been able to win the confidence of the two parties with regard to our impartiality, the neutrality of our relief operations, and the need for some form of accountability. We have convinced them that we're trying to be as even-handed as possible, the population in need being the determinant in the amount of supplies to be ferried in."

The structural bias of the UN system toward governments and the problems of coordination among UN agencies described earlier, however, suggest that the system itself is not yet properly structured to respond to such crises. Many of the senior UN officials associated with Lifeline believe that basic changes are needed. They differ primarily on where the expanded humanitarian mandate should be lodged and how it should relate to sovereignty, which governments show few signs of relinquishing.

"The mandate of the UN in dealing with humanitarian needs in armed conflict settings needs to be fully legitimized and further strengthened," says Michael Priestley. "We're pushing at the frontiers right now. The issue of national sovereignty in circumstances of extreme human suffering due to conflict should be examined at UN headquarters with a view to expanding the Secretary-General's powers." Under-Secretary-General Farah is currently soliciting the views of various UN agencies and officials as part of just such a review.

Grant, whom UN colleagues credit with "stretching the UN system internally" to deal with crises that would have been beyond their response capacity earlier on, is open to having the UNICEF mandate shared with other specialized agencies and to creating a new position such as an Under-Secretary-General for Special Humanitarian Affairs. A permanent office could avoid some of the blurred authority and accountability that Lifeline experienced. Yet with-

The United Nations Under Siege

The Sudan's civil war took a heavy toll on the UN. In the years just preceding Lifeline, two senior UN officials had left the country under duress for trying to help people in the south: Winston Prattley of UNDP in 1986 and Cole Dodge of UNICEF in 1989. A WFP consultant lost his life when a private relief plane was shot down in December 1989. An armed attack on the first UN relief train nearly cost UN lives. During the first year of Lifeline, some twenty persons employed by the UN, many of them drivers and others hired locally for Lifeline duties, were killed.

In a report to the UN General Assembly in September 1989, the Secretary-General saluted "the remarkable courage and determination of the drivers, their support crews and the United Nations/NGO escort teams. They have been confronted with mines, rocket attack and automatic weapons fire, all aimed at clearly marked United Nations convoys. The images of drivers killed and wounded, UN escort leaders targeted for assassination, and abandoned, burned-out relief vehicles offer a sobering appreciation of the human cost Operation Lifeline Sudan has incurred in some of its humanitarian efforts."[4]

out an action-oriented mandate, a new office might make humanitarian responses more subject to the political agendas of UN member states and more bureaucratic.

Sovereignty and Non-Governmental Organizations

NGOs providing relief aid in the Sudan tended to be less concerned about sovereignty, although as with matters political, their approaches were highly divergent. Some would agree with the Nairobi-based NGO executive who says, "I recognize Khartoum as much as the SPLA does." Others make it a rule to stay within applicable law, such as it is in civil war situations. NGOs in government-controlled areas work with the knowledge and consent of the Khartoum authorities. Those active in SPLA-controlled areas have obtained the consent of the insurgents and usually of the Kenyan government. Those who insist on strict legality would, apart from Lifeline, probably not have been able to work in SPLA territory at all.

Most NGOs are less respectful of sovereignty than are inter-governmental organizations because they express humanitarian concerns of their supporters that have strong moral underpinnings. Treating as enemies civilians who happen to find themselves in "enemy territory" is, from that vantage point, antithetical to basic humanitarian and moral principles.

NGOs tend to recognize the claims of sovereign political authorities only to the extent that they reflect humane values. Many do not acknowledge the Sudan government's claim, for example, to establish the terms under which they may provide assistance in SPLA-controlled areas. "If we allow sovereignty to affect delivery of relief," asks Taban Paride, Catholic Bishop of Torit, "then what are human rights?" On the other hand, if the authorities themselves allow humanitarian tasks to be performed, there is no need to challenge their sovereignty.

As for NGOs' own activities, "We are practitioners of what is possible," comments Emergency Coordinator Marcus Thompson of Oxfam-UK, "rather than what is legal."[5] That is not to say that NGO action takes place without reference to any norms whatsoever. It means only that NGO activities are not bound by what sovereign governments see fit to approve.

Médecins sans Frontières groups, whose name signals their unwillingness to allow political boundaries to limit humanitarian action, base their activities on the Universal Declaration of Human Rights. (See box, p. 86) They view the Declaration as imposing important limits on the unrestrained sovereignty of

Some of Lifeline's food was distributed to young children in feeding centers operated by private aid agencies. Pictured here is a supplementary feeding program in the town of Torit.

WFP/Jeff Share

states. "The actions of MSF rely on ethical rather than legal norms," explains Reginald Moreels, President of MSF-Belgium. "The actions that MSF undertakes could thus become lawful in their turn," which is to say, when the behavior of states more fully conforms to moral imperatives and to the various human rights conventions that many states have embraced.[6]

NGOs thus see themselves expanding the limits of humanitarian ethics rather than being constrained by existing law. "We know that there will be a long and difficult road to travel," says former President of the French NGO Médecins du Monde Bernard Kouchner, "before humanitarian organizations will finally be in a position to cross international borders unhindered, to treat and care for the ailing around the world. We hope, however, that our work will someday be carried out with the law on our side."[7] As French Minister for Humanitarian Affairs since 1988, Kouchner has lobbied for a new international convention that clearly defines not only the right of civilians to succor but also the right and even the duty of aid agencies to assist.

NGOs identified with these viewpoints can expect to be treated warily by governments within whose jurisdictions they operate. There was even some speculation that the MSF groups may have been targeted for violence in the Sudan precisely because of their outspoken views about sovereignty and suffering. Whatever the situation, however, a residue of bad feelings toward NGOs from the earlier famine has affected the government's perception of them during Lifeline. NGOs had descended on the Sudan in large numbers in 1984-85 and, in the view of the Khartoum authorities, conducted themselves as the sovereign authority in several northern provinces.

Again, there are critical differences in approaches to sovereignty between NGOs and the ICRC. "In planning emergency relief operations in situations of conflict," says Marcus Thompson, NGOs other than the ICRC, and "certainly we in Oxfam, act without conscious reference to international humanitarian law."[8] The ICRC, on the other hand, seeks to ground all of its actions clearly within such law.

Given these various views of the relevance of sovereignty and law to the relief of suffering, the request by Lifeline authorities, reasonable on its face, for NGOs to sign a Letter of Association raised serious problems.

NGOs and Sovereignty

As NGOs our hands are not tied by UN charters, rules, and regulations. One day perhaps the UN community will understand its limitations and start to cooperate with us in a true way. Unfortunately, tens of thousands of Sudanese, Salvadorans, Keren, Tigrayans, Eritreans, Angolans, and Lebanese will not live to witness that happy moment.

Jacques Willemse,
Head of Emergency and Refugees
Department, Dutch Interchurch Aid

Few NGOs have difficulty endorsing its principle that "emergency humanitarian assistance should be delivered to civilians" or that aid vehicles will carry only "relief supplies and personnel directly involved in relief operations."

Some, however, hesitate to agree to work fully under the Lifeline umbrella. They see the UN's requisite subservience to sovereignty endangering the humanitarian space that they credit Lifeline with having opened and sustained. Although refusal to sign the letter deprives them of access to Lifeline flights, to UN intercession with the recognized political authorities, and to resources mobilized by Lifeline, some NGOs have chosen to keep their boundary-free options open. They are not persuaded that UN authorities, having now entered into formal agreement with NGOs, will be more successful in protecting NGO activities from government intrusion.

In fact, it is in part the UN's difficulty in dealing with insurgent movements that has created more demand for NGO services, and therefore more visibility and vulnerability for them. Since "the legal orientation of most multilateral institutions remains that of establishing aid relationships with recognized governments," observes Barbara Hendrie, "NGOs are increasingly compelled to undertake aid relationships with 'non-recognized' movements, in order to fill the gap."[9] It is not surprising, then, that fundamentally different approaches to matters of sovereignty, politics, and morality should produce problems of association and coordination.

Sovereignty and Donor Governments

On issues pertaining to sovereignty, donor governments proved themselves *more* able to respond to suffering than the UN but *less* able than NGOs. In fact, the existence of Lifeline on the one hand and non-governmental channels on the other allowed bilateral aid agencies to pick and choose how they wished to assist those in need. The courses they charted were generally pragmatic, on occasion opportunistic, and sometimes inconsistent.

"When donors are at odds with the recipient government," observes Michael Priestley, "they tend to put most of their resources through NGOs and, at the same time, demand that the UN plays a central coordinating and monitoring role." As a result, "NGOs have been deliberately used in cross-border operations where governments are either unwilling or unable to become directly involved. In most circumstances they do this with the full realization of the much reduced accountability that inevitably accompanies a strictly illicit operation."

The activities of various Western governments, among them the US, demonstrate the point. During the years preceding

Lifeline, the US channeled aid to the Sudan largely through its Khartoum ally. As a result, it assisted people in government-controlled areas only. As the suffering worsened in 1988, US aid officials explored ways to help in SPLA-controlled areas, despite the fact that the US did not have a formal relationship with the insurgents.

For much of 1988, the US gave top priority to supporting ICRC efforts to negotiate an agreement with the protagonists, at the same time restraining UNICEF's wish to assist in SPLA areas. The US also provided food aid through NGOs operating from Kenya and Uganda to people in government-held towns. As the tragedy deepened and aid channels remained constricted, deference to the political sensitivities of the Khartoum authorities became increasingly untenable. "We were so riveted on the problem of sovereignty...," recalls Julia Taft, former Director of AID's Office of Foreign Disaster Assistance. "But a country's sovereignty doesn't give it the right to do what was happening in the Sudan."

In August 1988 Taft dispatched a "joint NGO/AID team" to Nairobi to assess needs in SPLA-controlled areas. The AID personnel went as far as Kenya; the NGO representatives proceeded into the southern Sudan. There was great uneasiness among US diplomats at the thought of US NGOs -- to say nothing of the US aid officials and itinerant members of Congress likely to follow -- setting foot inside SPLA-controlled areas. While the State Department expressed a natural concern for the safety of Americans in a war zone, its real fear seemed to be a backlash by the Khartoum government against US interests. The diplomatic establishment, strongly committed to sovereignty, was infuriated when Taft, equally committed to the relief of suffering, met with SPLM representative Mansour Khalid in late January 1989.

Throughout late 1988 and early 1989, recalls OFDA's William Garvelink, "We were very eager to find some way -- for example, a UN umbrella -- so that we could legitimize US government activities in the southern Sudan." With the new policy of the Bush administration in January to assist people on both sides and with the advent of Lifeline itself in March, the US for the first time could reach people across the political divide.

A year later, a three-person AID team, no longer using US NGOs as cover, made an "historic" one-month trip through SPLA-controlled areas. It was, the group reported with great enthusiasm, "the first voyage of an official American delegation

---

Sovereignty and Civil War

Civil wars with their train of violence and human suffering often place the United Nations in a difficult dilemma. The concept of the sovereignty of states prevents the UN from intervening in their internal affairs without the consent of the recognized government. On the other hand, the organization is committed to upholding human rights and humanitarian principles and cannot remain indifferent to the plight of the civilian population affected by civil war.

To skirt this dilemma, the Secretary-General of the United Nations may endeavor to set up a humanitarian operation in a country ravaged by civil war after securing, through moral suasion, the consent of the government in place. Such an operation must scrupulously avoid taking sides or interfering in any other way in the internal political struggle. But, in addition to providing the civilian population with much needed relief, it often has a moderating effect on the government and the anti-government forces in the civil war.

F.T. Liu
Former Assistant Secretary-General
for Special Political Affairs
United Nations

into the areas of the south" where the US had been funding Lifeline and NGO activities for more than a year. Prior to Lifeline, SPLA-controlled areas -- including the SRRA head-quarters itself -- had been off-limits to US government person-nel. After March 1989, the UN umbrella helped shield the US from political fallout.

With the beginning of Lifeline, then, the US was able to step up its resource commitments dramatically. It provided an array of contributions to Lifeline, including grants to enable UNICEF and WFP to hire additional staff on the scene. At the same time, the US increased its support of NGOs such as Catholic Relief Services, LWF, the International Rescue Commit-tee, Church World Service, World Vision, CARE, Mercy Corps International, Lutheran World Relief, Air Serv, the ICRC, and the League of Red Cross and Red Crescent Societies. It also provided resources to strengthen both the RRC on the govern-ment side and the SRRA on the insurgents' side.

European governments, too, found NGOs a convenient channel that spared them direct dealings with the protagonists. One government wishing to assist in *SPLA*-controlled areas without the knowledge of Khartoum made a grant for work in *govern-ment*-controlled areas to an NGO with activities on both sides. The understanding was that the NGO would use funds thus freed up to assist on the SPLA side. Lifeline rendered such subterfuge less necessary.

There was never much clarity, and sometimes not much consistency, in government funding of NGOs. Most govern-ments provided NGOs with resources for activities broadly consonant with Lifeline's objectives but without specifying any particular accountability to the UN. At the same time, as Priestley observed, governments expected the UN, which they also funded, to exercise overall coordination. As a result, governments put NGOs and the UN on a collision course and sometimes ended up supporting contradictory strategies.

Governments helped underwrite the LWF airlift which during a twenty-month period beginning in November 1988 transported over 25,000 tons of relief supplies from Nairobi to government-held Juba. In an effort to prevail upon the Sudan government to lift its ban on relief flights, the UN wanted LWF to suspend its flights too and asked the donor governments funding LWF to insist that it do so. (See box, p. 96) LWF, which has never considered its activities part of Lifeline, circumvented AID's directive and the UN's strategy by enlisting US congressional support to allow it to continue flying.

On some occasions the EC also funded NGO activities at variance with Lifeline, which it also supported. On others, the EC sought to line up NGO grantees squarely behind Lifeline and assure a more closely coordinated use of resources.

In more normal circumstances, governments would have funded activities by their own aid agencies in addition to those done on their behalf by the UN, NGOs, and the ICRC. Given the constraints imposed by the civil war, however, their options were more limited. Their use of intermediaries allowed them to help relieve suffering while finessing the problems of dealing directly with the insurgents. One government aid official voiced the views of others in observing, "There's no question that UN agencies and NGOs, one or another or both of them, on different occasions fronted for us."

Sovereignty and Responsibility

A common thread in Lifeline's struggle to come to terms with the tensions between sovereignty and suffering has been the difficulty experienced by most institutions -- governments, UN agencies, and NGOs alike -- in respecting the neutrality of humanitarian assistance. Providing or blocking such aid was constantly interpreted as a friendly or unfriendly -- that is to say, a political -- act.

"There does not seem to be an appreciation, understanding, experience, or willingness to accept the concept of the neutrality of humanitarian assistance," reflects Julia Taft. "This is partly because it is sometimes not really neutral and partly because it affects sovereignty and political interests."

Yet as understood in international law, humanitarian assistance is characterized precisely by its neutrality. Giving or receiving humanitarian assistance neither confers sovereignty nor erodes it. Protocol I of the Geneva Conventions of 1977 makes the essential point. "Offers of relief shall not be regarded as interference in the armed conflict or as unfriendly acts."[10] The OAU Refugee Convention stipulates that a government that accepts refugees from another African country is fulfilling a humanitarian obligation, not committing a hostile political act. The International Court of Justice held in 1986 that providing "strictly humanitarian assistance . . . cannot be regarded as unlawful intervention or as in any other way contrary to international law."[11] Ruling on a case brought by Nicaragua, the Court found that the so-called humanitarian assistance from the US government to the contras did not measure up to international standards for such aid.

One of the difficulties illuminated by the Sudan experience, however, is the weakness of the protections in current international law for civilian populations, particularly those displaced within a given country, and for those who wish to aid them. "The humanitarian law of armed conflict is still first and foremost a law of states," observes one expert. "Moreover, it is a law between states, rather than a law which is in fact above them and capable of being enforced by machinery provided or available for that purpose."[12] In the tension between sovereignty and suffering, sovereign states have the

Sovereignty and Humanity

Sovereignty need not conflict with humanitarian concerns if States can be brought to define their interests beyond the short term. Trimming the edges of sovereignty to allow for effective multilateralism does not imply undermining or superseding the State. The interests of common humanity which transcend national boundaries are not a menace to the vital interests of States.[13]

Independent Commission on International Humanitarian Issues

last word, resourceful humanitarian diplomacy notwithstanding.

A new and promising departure for the UN, Lifeline also illuminated the extent to which the UN remains captive to the traditional concept of sovereignty. While its Charter opens with the words "We, the peoples," the remaining operational articles are state-centric. In the Sudan crisis, the UN ignored for a time the appeals of the Sudanese people, of non-governmental (that is, people's) organizations, and even of its own staff. It was only after member governments insisted on it that Lifeline was launched. Urgent humanitarian need did not exercise an independent claim on UN action.

To its credit, the UN ultimately found ways of responding creatively to people trapped within Sudanese territory but beyond the reach of the Sudan government. Paradoxically, it was the UN that legitimized the involvement of donor governments in the crisis and opened up for member states new and expanded avenues for reaching such people. Of the major actors, the UN thus emerges from the Sudan experience as the most consistent respecter of sovereignty, even while working to infuse it with humanitarian content.

* * *

The clearest lesson of Lifeline in the area of sovereignty is summed up by Dr. Gazuli D'Faallah, Prime Minister of the Sudan in 1985-6 and currently chairman of the IARA board. "Within the accepted norms and definitions of national sovereignty," he observes, "people can help alleviate suffering. The solution to the tension between sovereignty and humanitarian concern is redefining the sovereignty issue. Within the sovereignty of states, all these humanitarian concerns can be addressed."

Dr. Gazuli would probably not agree with those who say that a government that fails to meet its responsibilities in the areas of humanitarian action and human rights forfeits its claim to have its sovereignty respected. A "use-it-responsibly" or "lose-it-entirely" approach to sovereignty would pose particular challenges in Africa, where many military dictatorships and some one-party states might resist such an orientation. However, as a global upsurge in more representative and responsive government makes itself felt, the position of African governments and the OAU may also change.

Sovereignty, however, imposes re-

A Sudanese youngster and a relief worker at a feeding center in Kapoeta in SPLA-controlled southeastern Sudan.
International Rescue Committee/Jenny Sulgar

sponsibilities on all governments, not just on those of poorer countries struggling with civil strife and grinding poverty. "You tell us we're breaking the laws of national sovereignty," charges Dr. Gazuli. "Why is it that now, because we are third world countries and because you want to help us, you ask us to waive our sovereignty? If the international community is so very concerned about human suffering," he asks with a touch of irony, "why then doesn't it look into the roots of the suffering? The countries requesting us to waive our sovereignty are partly responsible for our suffering. The suffering is caused by fighting, and people are fighting with modern arms. The modern arms are not manufactured in the Sudan."

The point is a serious one. International law imposes obligations on all parties, those who have acknowledged their duty to provide humanitarian assistance no less than those whose cooperation is being enlisted to allow it to be provided. All states party to the Geneva Conventions and Protocols are pledged to insist on their implementation. Moreover, mutual obligations in the area of humanitarian assistance are cut from a larger cloth of moral and legal commitments that member states and the international community have also embraced.

The Independent Commission on International Humanitarian Issues sees poorer nations rightly wondering: "Where was the outrage of the international community, whose norms we are now being asked to respect, during the crises that imprisoned us in poverty, ignorance and oppression, that killed our children through malnutrition and diseases, that despoiled our lands?" The rigors of everyday existence for most people in places like the Sudan mitigate against the development of some special allegiance to a set of international norms which make little apparent difference in their lives.

"The keen sense of structural violence on the part of its victims, and their determination to resist it," continues the Commission, "is the link that joins long-term issues of poverty and injustice to the breakdown of humanitarian norms in wars or violent internal struggles. The contenders in such struggles are not likely to observe the norms set by the international community until they are acknowledged to be a part of it themselves."[14]

* * *

In short, the concept of sovereignty, comprehensively understood, requires a change of perspective by all involved. Whether developed or developing, donor or host, governments of countries have unfinished business in this area. So, too, do political authorities, whether military or democratic, single party or multi-party, established regimes or insurgencies. While practices in developing countries that place humanitarianism under siege are blatant and offensive, the failures of developed countries to meet their own humanitarian obligations, broadly understood, are no less serious.

Forces of change sweeping across the globe are now calling into question the traditional concept of sovereignty and the arbitrary national borders and unrepresentative political structures it is frequently invoked to protect. The Lifeline experience suggests that responsibly exercised, sovereignty can go hand-in-hand with more effective efforts to alleviate suffering.

Chapter 5
Relief and Peace

The time has come for us in the Horn of Africa to ask whether the efforts of relief agencies are contributing, indirectly or even remotely, to an escalation of the wars or to a peaceful resolution of the conflicts.

Dr. Kibiru Kinyanjui
Peace Activist, March 1990

Many who had hoped and expected that Lifeline would bring peace are sharply critical of it for having failed to do so. They acknowledge that Lifeline succeeded in reducing hostilities for a time and in facilitating the safe passage of relief supplies. However, after a few short months, the warring parties were back at their bloody struggle, fortified by the reprieve Lifeline had provided. Whatever short-term tranquility Lifeline may have afforded, according to this view, it left untouched the roots of the long-standing conflict.

They have a point. If Lifeline were only about moving commodities, it would not be much different from other relief operations. In fact, Lifeline's 100,000-plus tons seem modest indeed compared to the 900,000 tons of food being rushed to northern Ethiopia, Eritrea, and Tigray in 1990. While the movement of relief during a civil war sets Lifeline apart from more typical disaster relief programs, providing aid in civil wars is not altogether unprecedented either. Lifeline would have a special claim to fame, however, if it had arranged to surround relief efforts with tranquility or, better yet, had brought into being a lasting peace.

The interplay between relief and peace is perhaps the most intriguing and complex aspect of the entire initiative. While

Lifeline did not end the war, it encouraged dialogue and provided a point of agreement when division prevailed virtually everywhere else. Lifeline also illuminated the links between human suffering, on the one hand, and the ongoing war, the continuing abuses of human rights, and chronic poverty on the other. As a result, the relevance of humanitarian assistance to peace, respect for human rights, and broad-based development has become more indisputable, even if Lifeline itself did not tackle that broader agenda.

Peace appears no closer in mid-1990 than before Lifeline began. In fact, the warring parties may be even farther apart. Clearly, cooperation on the humanitarian challenge has proved insufficient to guarantee progress on more divisive issues. The moral of the tale is not, however, that future relief should be conditioned on the prior resolution of the war. It is rather that relief and peace need to be pursued in tandem and with at least equal energy.

Great Expectations, Early Successes

With the launching of Lifeline, hopes for peace in the Sudan soared. After the frustration of relief efforts for so many years, the agreement represented a breakthrough in a region where fratricidal war had been the norm and reconciliation the exception. "There is, at long last, good news from Sudan," wrote Abdul Mohammed in *The Washington Post* of May 25, 1989. "Emergency food is being moved, albeit slowly, to the war-ravaged south. A repeat of the catastrophic famine that last year claimed the lives of an estimated quarter million people is likely to be averted."

Mohammed went on to say that Lifeline "has set a precedent of trust in a region scarred by murderous civil war. It has engineered cooperation between combatants who in the past have used food aid as a weapon. Hope has been wrested from tragedy. Humanitarian concern [has] outgunned the exigencies of war. This invaluable precedent should not be wasted."

The optimism regarding peace was widely shared. To be sure, Lifeline was attempting the well-nigh impossible. "But optimism is what this whole operation is about," reported Gill Lusk in the *Middle East International* magazine shortly after Lifeline's debut, "optimism that [Lifeline] will succeed in keeping alive a significant number of the hundreds of thousands of starving or near starving civilians. And optimism that it will bring opportunities to reinforce the existing peace process."[1]

Peace was very much in the air in Khartoum in March 1989, both inside and outside the hall where Lifeline was being launched. Referring to the agreement reached the previous November in Addis Ababa, the head of the Canadian delegation told the gathering, "We deeply regret that the serious opportunity for peace which emerged in November has been left in abeyance while innocent civilians continue to suffer and die."

"We welcome the formation of a new national government which is committed to a peace process," he continued. "We appeal to that government and to the SPLA to dedicate themselves to finding a durable solution to the conflict which is devastating the south." Looking to the relief task, he pledged that "Canada, for its part, will continue to support international humanitarian efforts to assist the victims of the situation." Beyond relief, however, progress in conflict resolution would be key to Canada's future interaction with the Sudan. "In the absence of a peace settlement and national reconciliation we will consider seriously whether continuing assistance of other than a purely humanitarian nature can be justified."

Canada's careful statement stopped short of threatening a cut-off of future *humanitarian* assistance in the absence of progress to end the war. Yet it made clear that the fundamental issue needing attention, and the obstacle to the resumption of normal relationships, was the conflict itself. Other governments less prepared to tackle the issue head-on thanked the Canadians privately for drawing the connection. Lifeline, they hoped, would represent a confidence-building measure on the basis of which peace could be pursued and achieved.

Early success in forcing the fighting to make room for relief was encouraging. When both protagonists rejected the initial UN proposal for a six-month cease-fire, the UN countered by proposing a single month of tranquility throughout the south that the SPLA found too all-embracing. Both sides finally agreed on certain "corridors of tranquility" through which, during an initial month, clearly identified relief supplies would be granted safe passage. (See map, p. 30) This arrangement was extended month by month until the war broke out again in late October.

Lifeline thus succeeded in establishing an effective buffer around relief activities. The results were both less and more constructive than UN officials had envisioned. While safe passage did become a reality for aid moving through the corridors, whether by land, river, or air, only five of the eight corridors saw regular use. Political, military, and security considerations narrowed the number through which relief could routinely pass.

On the more positive side, rather than providing simply "bubbles" of protection for individual relief vehicles passing through the stated areas, the protagonists declared the corridors themselves off-limits to all military operations. The SPLA declared a cease-fire that lasted from May through mid-June, the government a unilateral truce for July that it extended through August and then September. The value to relief operations, combined with the international approbation received, became factors in protecting and extending the arrangements.

Strictly speaking, the cease-fire and truces applied only to the corridors of tranquility, with the protagonists keeping their options open to fight elsewhere. However, the return of tranquility to the corridors helped reclaim for civilian use the roads, which were the main arteries for overland military movements. Commerce which had thrived before the war along the roads began to flourish again, benefiting the surrounding countryside as well. With the perceptible decrease in tension and upswing in market activity, the enlarged corridors became, in effect, zones of peace.

Thus the protection of relief activities became a step toward a broader de-escalation of the conflict, even though the protagonists were still free to fight outside the corridors and to suspend the arrangements unilaterally whenever they chose. "The cease-fire was a happy outcome of Lifeline which we really didn't expect," observes Lifeline's southern sector operations chief, Vincent E. O'Reilly. It was, he says, "almost an accidental by-product."

While the corridors of tranquility and their related arrangements facilitated relief activities, both protagonists went to great lengths to distinguish between the two. "There was no relation between relief and the cease-fires," insists SPLA Commander Riak Macar. "The fact that we did not fight for three months was our decision. The reasons for the cease-fires were political and had nothing to do with relief." His Khartoum counterparts say the same.

The distinction, which seemed like hair-splitting to some, had a purpose. The protagonists sought to distinguish their commitments to safe passage for relief from their more general suspension of fighting in the corridors. Agreeing to corridors of tranquility was a specific action taken in the interests of humanitarian relief; suspending military operations was a broader political decision.

The distinction also reflected their desire to keep options open to resume fighting. The parties did not want a resumption of the war to trigger a cessation of relief. The corridors would remain open to relief activities, they said, whether or not the war was rekindled. Privately, however, the parties conceded that the political steps they had taken were themselves designed to facilitate relief. Dr. Lam Akol, a high-ranking SPLM/A official, is quoted as referring to Lifeline as "the catalyst in bringing about the cease-fire."[2]

The warring parties were also anxious to establish that the decisions regarding cease-fires and truces had been taken on their own, not under coercion from outsiders. The parties are well known to each other and "don't need any external pressure to bring them to the realization that the war has been very destructive," the Sudan's Ambassador to the United States Abdalla Ahmed Abdalla pointed out in March 1990. "The Sudan government realizes very well that this is a war which is not needed and should stop. It is a war which has caused tremendous damage to all the people of the Sudan, particularly in the south." In short, the critical issue for the protagonists was not the war but rather "how to find common grounds for peace."

Humanitarianism And Causes

We do not identify with partisan causes. We identify with and respond to human needs. At the same time, we try to understand what the causes imply for the people. Each is legitimate, each has its own life.

William Reimer,
Mennonite Central Committee

Relief activities provided such common grounds. While the protagonists had agreed well before Lifeline to allow food to reach civilians on both sides, Lifeline gave them a vehicle to transform principle into policy and then finally into program and practice.

Contributions toward peace notwithstanding, Lifeline was not a peace initiative. James Grant recalls that "there was nothing in my mandate at all" as far as resolving the conflict was concerned. While he and other Lifeline officials fervently hoped that the initiative would contribute to peace and were distressed when violence recurred, they did not see peace as an explicit or necessary part of Lifeline's purpose or justification.

On an early visit to Khartoum, Grant turned aside a request from the SCC to use Lifeline as the basis for a UN peace effort. Ezekiel Kutjok, the SCC's General Secretary, recalls that Grant distinguished between the capacity of the UN to provide relief and the use of the same access to negotiate peace. The kind of peace process that had proved successful elsewhere around the world, Grant said, would require a formal invitation to the Secretary-General from the government. One had not been -- and still has not been -- received.

Grant nevertheless believes that Lifeline indirectly advanced the peace process. He recalls el Mahdi's displeasure that during the early weeks of Lifeline, fighting had intensified outside the corridors of tranquility. The Prime Minister, like Grant, apparently had hopes that ranged beyond relief.

Strictly speaking, then, Lifeline cannot be faulted for not accomplishing what it was not explicitly charged with doing. At the same time, it fell short of its potential by not capitalizing on the possibilities for peace that it reflected and helped create. In retrospect, Lifeline's mandate seems unnecessarily narrow.

Creating An Environment for Peace

Disavowing a Lifeline mandate to end the war, James Grant nonetheless believes that Lifeline played a role in creating "an environment for peace." The evidence bears him out. Lifeline both helped create such an environment and benefited from it.

The corridors of tranquility and their reinforcing political arrangements were critical to Lifeline's success. "How do you do relief when there is no cease-fire?" asks Brigadier Pio Yukwan Deng, one of the southerners on the current Revolutionary Command Council. "The corridors of tranquility were a sort of experiment," he muses, looking back. "They have saved so many lives."

In addition to their logistical benefits, the corridors had psychological value as well. People in the streets of Juba and throughout the rural south saw relief activities as a harbinger of peace. "The fact that the planes were flying gave people the hope that they could live," recalls Robert H. Brandstetter, the senior UN official in Juba in late 1989, "and that some kind of peace could come about." That hope contrasted sharply with cries of despair emanating from the Bishop of Wau in the period before Lifeline and from the Bishop of Torit during Lifeline when no relief supplies were reaching their areas. Humanitarian activity contributed directly to people's sense of confidence and security.

Lifeline also stimulated dialogue on the issues underlying the conflict. A Sudanese who helped persuade Prime Minister Sadiq el Mahdi to endorse Lifeline recalls that "the international community saw Lifeline as creating a favorable atmosphere for peace in this country. We Sudanese saw it as a call for reason: this war is doing tremendous damage and needs to be stopped." Lifeline, in short, could serve to generate momentum toward peace through relief. The fact that the

Prime Minister's confidant now requests anonymity suggests the extent to which peace activism and advocacy for humanitarian assistance have once again become risky endeavors.

In addition to helping create conditions conducive to peace, Lifeline itself was possible because of a climate in which peace was becoming an increasingly serious option. A series of political developments over a period of years had prepared the ground for Lifeline's acceptance.

Since as early as 1986, relief assistance to civilians had been an explicit part of the agenda of peace groups and a number of northern political parties. The major political hurdle had always been a lack of trust and organizational commitment. For a series of governments, implementing a pledge to provide such aid had proved difficult. Ruling coalitions were fragile, with some individuals and parties more committed to assistance than others. Government ministries were disorganized and vulnerable to forces opposed to providing aid to "rebels" in the south. The insurgents lacked mechanisms for implementing an aid program and had a basic mistrust of the Khartoum authorities.

Late in 1988 and early in 1989, an increasingly strong constituency for peace was emerging and asserting itself, even in the military. In November, as the UN General Assembly was debating the deteriorating humanitarian situation, representatives of the Democratic Union Party and trade unions were meeting with the SPLM/A in Addis Ababa to hammer out the principles for peace negotiations.

The Addis "peace agreement" changed the atmosphere markedly and provided the necessary, if not the sufficient, conditions for continued negotiations leading to its acceptance by the Sudan government. As the Prime Minister hesitated to endorse the agreement, a mid-February ultimatum from the army gave him a week to commit himself to it and to form a more broadly based government. By mid-March he had made that commitment and had chosen a new cabinet, broadly representative except for the absence of the NIF, which wanted the war prosecuted more vigorously. At just the time when concrete evidence of good faith in the peace process was needed, Lifeline offered both sides a way of demonstrating their sincerity.

During the next three months -- the make-or-break period for Lifeline -- a realignment of the ruling coalition strengthened the forces committed to peace. At the same time, the NIF campaigned against both peace and the relief initiative. On June 29, 1989 the National Peace Committee formed in March succeeded in getting the Prime Minister's agreement to the peace proposals, including, for the first time, the freezing of *sharia* and the granting of amnesty to those arrested for violating it. Before el Mahdi could enlist the expected endorsement of his cabinet, however, he was overthrown by a coup on June 30. The plotters had acted, they said, to halt the "signing of the document of surrender," meaning the five-point plan for bringing a negotiated peace to the Sudan.

From the perspective of domestic politics, then, Lifeline benefited from the growing sense that relief and peace needed to be pursued more vigorously and more in concert. The fact that Lifeline became an NIF target confirms its close and serious association with peace. But again, Lifeline the beneficiary of the political climate was also, in a reinforcing way, a contributor to dialogue. In difficult negotiations between the Sudan government and the SPLM/A, Lifeline helped the parties maintain communication when relief was about the only thing they could agree on.

One participant recalls that on several occasions when the peace negotiations threatened to collapse, agreement on humanitarian aid saved the day. One such session was about to break up in disarray when a government official proposed as a last resort that both sides reaffirm their commitment to assure relief to all in need. After all, he said, those who are suffering are "not strangers but our own children." Moved by the appeal, SPLM officials stated that they, too, were committed to the children of the Sudan. Common ground was rediscovered.

In historical context, the view of some UN officials that Lifeline itself was the basis for initiating peace talks is inaccurate. However, Lifeline can take credit for having contributed to an atmosphere conducive to peace. Persons on each side of the

---

A Veteran of Sieges

The most well-established humanitarian assistance agency in situations of internal armed conflict is the International Committee of the Red Cross. Founded in 1863 and based in Geneva, Switzerland, it has contributed to the evolution of international humanitarian law and is recognized by name in the Geneva Conventions and Protocols.

Obtaining the agreement of the warring parties, standard operating procedure for the ICRC, proved unusually difficult in the Sudan. The ICRC made a formal proposal to both sides in early March 1988. Although the SPLM/A replied favorably two weeks later and the Sudan government in May, negotiation of common ground rules took until early December. In the interim, suffering among civilians reached an all-time high.

Lifeline built on the ICRC agreement. At the same time, Lifeline generated additional resources for ICRC activities, which included programs of feeding, health, and agriculture. While coordinating its work with Lifeline, the ICRC kept its distance from the UN and NGOs, accepting funds from governments, national Red Cross and Red Crescent societies, and the general public but not from the UN. During 1989, when the Sudan represented its largest program, the ICRC was active in forty three other countries.

conflict have praised Lifeline for having brought out the best in both sides. "Lifeline showed the possibility of putting some wisdom and reason into this conflict," said a Khartoum peace activist looking back in July 1990.

Illustrating the complexity of humanitarian action, military officials themselves on occasion viewed relief as a force for peace. The Defense Minister, retired General Abd al-Majid Hamid Khalil, whose resignation in mid-February 1989 over the Prime Minister's languid peace pace preceded the army's ultimatum by a single day, is credited with having encouraged the ICRC effort in 1988 to work out a relief agreement acceptable to both sides. He foresaw a visible Red Cross presence combining with resettlement and reconstruction aid to help defuse tension, rebuild confidence, and presage peace.

General Bashir, brought to power by the June coup, also gives cautious credit to Lifeline in the area of confidence-building. Interviewed in April 1990, he observed that "One of the major factors that motivates the continuation of the war is the lack of confidence and trust between the warring parties. An operation like Lifeline -- a situation in which you have relief moving across battle lines -- might help by building a foundation of trust between the protagonists."

Lifeline also served as a rallying point for humanitarian interests and concerns. People in the government and the SPLA, in the army and the political parties, in the press and among the public, all took heart. Lifeline responded to calls that the SPLM/A had been making since 1985 when it had set up the SRRA to serve as such a focal point for relief. Lifeline also became an RRC ally although, as indicated earlier, the relationship became something of a mixed blessing for the RRC.

In a general sense, the entire range of aid activities broadly associated with Lifeline fostered an environment conducive to peace. The involvement of the UN itself, however, had special importance. The UN's Robert H. Brandstetter recalls that during tense times in Juba in late 1989, "the UN presence gave everyone in government -- the mayor of Juba, regional government officials, teachers, and civil servants -- a sense that the world hadn't forgotten them." Ordinary citizens, too, knew about Lifeline, he remembers. "They felt that if the UN were involved, somebody was working towards peace."

* * *

Lifeline also contributed to a fuller appreciation of the complex interconnections between peace, human rights, and development. "There continued to be serious human rights violations in Sudan in 1988, stemming primarily from the civil war," the US State Department had reported the following year. "Until late in the year, elements of the competing forces frequently interfered or failed to cooperate with international relief efforts in order to gain advantage in the civil war. As a result of such interference, and of government negligence or inefficiency, many displaced persons suffered from severe malnutrition, and there were many deaths due to starvation and disease."[3]

By contrast, a report by Amnesty International covering the year 1989 credits "cease-fires declared by the government and the SPLA, combined with a massive United Nations effort to get food into famine affected areas in the south" with contributing to a significant reduction in human rights violations. Fewer violations both reflected a downturn in the war and contributed to a relaxation of tensions. Conversely, Amnesty International also reports an upswing in human rights violations on both sides in late 1989 and in 1990, again confirming the synergism in the relationship.[4]

If human rights violations were a product of the war and also fueled the conflict, greater protection of human rights was essential to a more stable and just future. "Resolution of conflicts and economic development in Africa will be most meaningful only if they are complemented by corresponding progress on human rights," OAU Secretary-General Salim Salim told the Council of Ministers in February 1990. "Such progress can be brought about through deliberate action by governments to take legislative measures and put into place structures and institutions aimed at enhancing and integrating the protection of human rights into the fabric of the African political process."[5]

A similar interplay was evident between peace and development. The tranquility associated with Lifeline, as noted earlier, stimulated commerce and brightened prospects for the future. The government's June 1990 bombing of Torit had the opposite effect. With people who had returned to the town as a statement of their faith in the future scattering back to the safer countryside, the process of moving beyond the emergency was delayed.

But if tranquility was needed for development, development was also an investment in peace. Aid practitioners see the need to approach development activities in countries experiencing ongoing civil strife as "conflict mitigation mechanisms." Peter Schumann, Chief of UNDP's Emergency Unit in Khartoum in late 1988 and early 1989, notes that "Development activities cannot be seen in isolation from conflicts. They are not neutral. They are interventions which can create or stimulate conflict, or help reduce and solve conflict."

The link between development and peace impelled much of the effort associated with Lifeline to move as quickly as possible beyond relief to reconstruction and development. "Relief and reconstruction activities," observes the Rev. Samuel Kobia, General Secretary of the National Council of Churches of Kenya -- and he might have added development as well -- are themselves "part of the search for justice and peace. Justice and peace cannot thrive in a vacuum. There has to be a social and economic set-up within which peace can prevail."

"There is a sort of circle here," say students of these inter-relationships at the global level, and the Sudan experience bears out their conclusion. "Development cannot be achieved without peace; without development, human rights are illusory; and peace without human rights is violence."[6] The interconnections suggest that agencies specializing in one particular area, whether humanitarian assistance, peace, human rights, or development, need to be more catholic in their concerns, even if their programs retain a more specialized focus.

With some of these connections in mind, UN officials are formulating plans to keep Lifeline in place for the next several years. The presence of Lifeline staff throughout the south would provide an early warning system against future food shortages and recurrent human rights abuses. Continued Lifeline activities to speed the rebuilding of basic economic and social infrastructure would act as something of a hedge against the outbreak of renewed bloodshed, helping prevent what one official calls "backsliding into chaos." The continuation of Lifeline, however, would require resources which, without the dramatic challenge from which the original Lifeline benefited, may prove more difficult to generate.

Summing up the interrelationships between relief and peace, Charles Kulundu, former foreign editor of the *Kenya Times*, observes that "Lifeline was a very vital contribution towards peace." While its activities stopped short of addressing the underlying causes of the suffering, Lifeline illuminated the fundamental problem. "When you talk the humanitarian language," adds Francis Deng, "you always end up talking about the war, which is the cause of all this suffering. The humanitarian agenda and the peace agenda are thus inherently connected."

Lifeline and the Continuing War

Did Lifeline prolong the conflict? Did the availability of relief, rather than bringing the warring parties together, contribute to continued bloodshed?

"The reason we're in need of help *is* this conflict," comments Dr. Gazuli D'Faallah, the former Prime Minister. "Everyone is very worried that the aid not be a way of perpetuating it." "We need to ponder," elaborates peace activist Kibiru Kinyanjui, "whether the services relief agencies provide make them partners in the wars by enabling fighters to fight the wars out in more protracted fashion."

Many hold that relief efforts in the Sudan have indeed fueled the underlying war. "Of course food prolonged the war," says an NGO official in Nairobi. "It provided food stocks for both sides. It allowed the SPLA to pacify potential opposition. It protected both warring parties from their citizens." And if further evidence is needed, it is readily available. "Relief is still being provided, and the war is still continuing."

The conclusion that Lifeline is to blame for the resumption of the conflict is questionable. Many of the moves away from peace by the warring parties might have been made with or without the presence of the relief program. In a broader sense, however, relief may indeed be linked to the continuing war. Certainly, each side used the respite to gird up for resumed battle. The government landed troops in Juba, along with provisions to keep them alive. The SPLA consolidated its hold throughout the rural south, benefiting in the process from its association with the relief Lifeline provided.

The availability of food aid also eased the need of both sides to care for their civilian populations, although based on the 1988 experience there is no guarantee that they would have provided the needed sustenance on their own. The fungibility of aid also meant that even if large amounts of food commodities themselves did not fall into the hands of the opposing armies, relief food indirectly benefited the warring parties.

The interplay among various factors reviewed earlier was such that humanitarian considerations in and of themselves could not be counted on to dictate the policies of the protagonists. Such concerns were generally respected only to the extent that they converged with perceived political and military interests. Thus Lifeline should not be held responsible for failing to prevent the outbreak of renewed violence in late 1989. It can be faulted, however, for not having been more resourceful in mobilizing the various domestic and international interests already associated with it to protect its ongoing humanitarian activities and to become a more insistent force for peace.

Interestingly, the protagonists themselves express a certain disappointment with Lifeline in this regard. "We look at peace as a process," observes the Sudan's Ambassador Abdalla. "You start with a cease-fire and corridors of tranquility and then take another step . . . gradually getting to the point of resolving political differences." What Lifeline failed to provide, he believes, was "a continued and sustained process [leading to] political negotiations to settle the conflict altogether."

The SPLM/A, too, regretted the lack of sustained pressure by Lifeline for peace. It blamed the government for the suspension of relief flights, ridiculing the assertion that the UN was smuggling arms to the SPLA as "an absurd accusation [with] no foundation whatsoever." Yet it made no secret of its view that the UN had not challenged the government's action forcefully enough. "Public denunciations of such an affront to the UN were muted," it observed in a sharply worded press release. "Only the SPLM/SPLA put its point of view across loud and clear that the Khartoum government was bent on blackmail, pure and simple."[7]

Despite the acrimony, protestations of interest in peace abounded on both sides throughout most of Lifeline. In September and October 1989, the government with some fanfare convened a national peace dialogue in Khartoum to address peace issues and dispatched abroad a delegation from the conference to publicize the interest in peace. General Bashir himself traveled in early 1990 to various countries in Africa and the Middle East to explore possibilities, he said, for dialogue with the insurgents.

The SPLM, which did not feel included in the Khartoum peace dialogue and did not take it seriously, often affirmed its own commitment to peace. "The cease-fire is open-ended as long as humanitarian needs remain," Commander Garang had said in September 1989, although the SPLA did not formally extend it beyond June. In his own missions to other countries, Garang stressed the SPLM's interest in ending the conflict. Yet Lifeline never became a vehicle for direct discussions of the political differences that divided the protagonists.

In an effort to build on the expressed interest in peace, former US President Jimmy Carter in December 1989 brought together representatives of the warring parties for talks in Nairobi. The meeting, which had the active support of Kenya's President Daniel Arap Moi, sought to address the religious and political differences contributing to the ongoing war. The overall climate at the time was negative, however, and the talks did not succeed in narrowing the differences.

While the UN did not itself undertake a peace initiative, it did struggle to find ways of making its relief activities less vulnerable to random or targeted violence. Early on James Grant examined the possibility, originally suggested by an NGO, of using a military or police contingent of humanitarian protection troops under UN auspices to provide limited protection for UN convoys using the agreed-upon corridors of tranquility. Swedish authorities were approached regarding

To beat the rains, Lifeline made heavy use of air transport.
WFP food is unloaded at an airstrip from a plane provided
by the government of the Federal Republic of Germany.
WFP/Jeff Share

making available a civil defense unit for that purpose. They
declined unless the UN Security Council authorized such an
undertaking. As the UN Secretariat believed that action by
the Security Council was unlikely and with time of the essence,
Grant dropped the proposal.

Reaction has been quite divided in the Sudan and elsewhere,
however, as to both the theory and the practice of providing
armed support for humanitarian operations. Some believe the
integrity of humanitarian assistance would be compromised if
force, however minimal, were used. Moreover, a number of
UN officials involved in the Sudan convoy operations, including W. Bryan Wannop whose life was threatened by the attack
on the Aweil train, have suggested that UN troops might
themselves have become a target. Grant himself sees the value
of such a contingent as that of "an international plate glass

window," functioning more as a deterrent than as a military force per se.

* * *

The interplay of relief and peace in the Sudan suggests that warring parties should not be given, nor should they be led to expect, carte blanche where humanitarian assistance is concerned. While humanitarian aid needs to be dependable, its providers should not allow it to be taken for granted. They need to be clearer among themselves and with the protagonists about the terms and conditions under which such aid loses its integrity and under which they themselves will no longer provide it. Joint strategies are important.

The expulsions of some aid agencies and personnel from the Sudan underscore the necessity for receiving and retaining the consent of the political authorities if humanitarian aid is to be provided at all. Conversely, however, the voluntary, if reluctant, exit of some aid agencies from the Sudan dramatizes the fact that there may be circumstances under which simply providing humanitarian assistance -- no questions asked -- can itself be a violation of humane values. (See box, p. 145)

Through and beyond the aid provided, relief initiatives like Lifeline need to work more diligently to counteract the dynamic in bitter civil strife that leads protagonists to stop at nothing to achieve their objectives. "When a man has placed his own life on the line and is prepared to kill or die for a cause," observes Francis Deng, "it is difficult for him to be overly concerned about the humanitarian needs of those who have remained behind the enemy lines, especially if that would compromise the cause for which he has chosen to make the ultimate sacrifice." The same could be said of a political authority that brings about the death of people within its own jurisdiction in the pursuit of its own political objectives.

Awareness that humanitarian aid will be pressed into the service of warring parties means that aid agencies should no longer understand their mission as that of simply keeping people alive. While humanitarian assistance is by definition, and should remain in practice, devoid of political, religious, military and other extraneous agendas, its provision in situations of armed conflict such as the Sudan's stands as an implicit judgment on the conflict itself.

Sometimes that judgment needs to be made explicit, as it was by the Canadian delegate at the Khartoum conference that launched Lifeline. He told the government that while donors would continue to make available humanitarian assistance, such aid was no substitute for resolving the strife that necessitated outside help. In fact, resolving the strife was of such importance that humanitarian considerations would be accorded greater

Tough Choices For Humanitarians

Many NGOs are currently considering closing or reducing operations due to increasingly difficult conditions, rapidly expanding costs, and increased harassment which combine to create a non-conducive, non-productive, non-sustainable situation. The line between the difficult and the impossible has been crossed. Many NGOs are now assessing this situation and arriving at similar conclusions.

There is undoubtedly a very difficult, complex decision point where one must weigh the benefits of the services provided against the overall cost and possibility of delivering them. This type of cost/benefit analysis is especially difficult when people's survival is at stake. We would all like to believe that we could "bear any burden, pay any price" but in reality we cannot. It is sad and tragic that the rural poor will lose the beneficial services we have provided.

Internal report explaining an NGO's decision to terminate Sudan activities Khartoum, January 1990

importance than was normally the case in the dealings of governments with each other.

Peace activist Kibiru Kinyanjui states the issue even more succinctly. "There needs to be a message to the fighters from those providing humanitarian assistance," he says. "Yes, we will supply the food. But there is something lacking in your own approach: a concern for peace." The need for an unequivocal statement to that effect -- and for policies to back it up -- is perhaps the quintessential message of Lifeline.

The positive effects of commodities and personnel that Lifeline introduced into the southern Sudan suggest the potential of humanitarian assistance to expand and transform the space within which it is provided. While Lifeline may have failed the ultimate challenge of bringing peace, there is a great deal to be learned from the difficulties it encountered. And whatever the disappointments in the area of peace, they should not detract from Lifeline's operational contributions.

A Higher Priority for Peace

Lifeline's role in helping to create an environment for peace and its uneasy relationship to the continuing war suggest a number of lessons to be learned from the Sudan experience as a whole.

First, however impressive the accomplishments of Lifeline as a relief operation, the delivery of supplies, indispensable though it be, is ultimately not its most important contribution. Food and other emergency supplies will seldom reach all in need, however determined those involved. The cessation of violence, on the other hand, benefits all. It allows civilian populations that ultimately must provide for themselves to begin to do so, whether or not they are reached with outside aid. The temptation to let logistical preoccupations dwarf what are ultimately more important benefits needs to be resisted.

Ironically, the renewal of Lifeline in March 1990 in Khartoum evidenced less rather than more

> ## Modern Wars
>
> There are fewer wars now than ten years ago but they are for the most part protracted internal conflicts with incredible brutalization of innocent civilians.
>
> Charles LaMuniere, senior UN official associated with Lifeline

attention to conflict resolution than a year earlier. "We are all aware," British Ambassador John Beavan told the Sudanese authorities on behalf of the donor governments, "that the suffering . . . will not really come to an end until peace is achieved." Yet few connections were drawn between the provision of aid and the resolution of the conflict.

To Lifeline's credit, its second phase has paid more attention to reconstruction and development needs. The tonnages of food assistance proposed for 1990 have been reduced below those in 1989, with planning figures for 1991 lower still. The absence of a higher priority for peace has reflected less an oversight on the part of donor governments than the hard-edged tenor of relationships between the warring parties and the more negative climate in which the relief initiative is set.

Second, Lifeline's lack of progress on the peace front reflects certain limitations inherent in relief itself. Lifeline 1 did not attempt to address the fundamental problem of the war, observes John Gachie, foreign editor of Nairobi's *The Nation* in early 1990, because "It could not take sides." The need for aid agencies to maintain the confidence of both sides, a task requiring scrupulous neutrality, clashes with their need to challenge both sides to find political solutions to their differences. In this sense, delivering aid and negotiating peace are separate and distinct endeavors.

Third, relief, despite its limitations, can nudge open the door for peace, though it cannot hold it open forever. Julia Taft sought to focus attention on the need for a negotiated settlement by suggesting a meeting of donor governments in advance of the 1989 Khartoum conference to clarify the linkage and to assure that it was acted upon while the relief program proceeded. Her suggestion was not adopted.

"Let's bring together the leadership of the Sudan government and of the SPLA," she remembers having urged. "Let's get the UN there. Let's get whoever is supplying the funds for these different wars there. Let's figure out a strategy so that you're not going to have just the humanitarian activity but also a political effort complementing it." The results were disappointing. "There was no international entity or donor," she recalls, "willing to try to use Lifeline as an opportunity for public diplomatic efforts. There was never energy placed on the peace side that I saw."

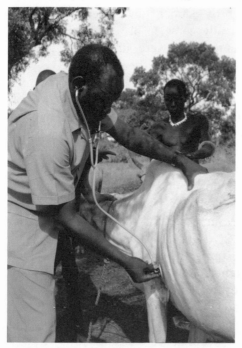

A Red Cross veterinarian examines a cow in a cattle camp in the district of Yirol in September 1989. ICRC/A. Grimm

The responsibility within the UN for such diplomatic efforts is lodged with the Secretary-General or his Under-Secretary-General for Special Political Questions, Abdulrahim A. Farah. Farah, who led the negotiations of the two Lifeline agreements, believes, as James Grant told the SCC in 1989, that without an invitation from the government, there is little that the UN can do to press for peace. The absence of peace and the continuing presence of relief, however, lends urgency to Taft's plea that "Next time, the donors should also agree to work strenuously on a peace process." That in fact was the pattern in Afghanistan, where UN-coordinated relief activities under Operation Salam were paralleled by UN-facilitated peace negotiations.

Certainly the working relationships necessary for successful relief operations should have positive spin-offs for cooperation on trickier political issues, although that did not happen in Lifeline. "In my judgment," says Randolph C. Kent, head of UNDP's emergency unit in Khartoum, "there's been no habit of cooperation formed. In fact, perhaps the reverse has happened: by forcing people to accept positions they don't agree with, Lifeline may have made genuine comity more difficult."

Finally, the Lifeline experience suggests that peace must be the preoccupation of all those committed to humanitarian values. To be sure, the UN has a special and indispensable role to play. However, governments, including those not "donors" to programs like Lifeline, have diplomatic and economic relationships that can serve as points of entry into the mediation process. In this respect, a more genuinely international and multilateral program, involving Arab and Muslim governments in a major way, would have made for more effective linkages between relief and diplomacy.

There are also crucial roles for NGOs to play. In the Sudan where religion is an element in the continuing strife, religious groups may have more limited roles than elsewhere. It is difficult to envision the churches, for example, playing as decisive a role as in 1972 when they mediated the peace talks that brought an end to the earlier civil war. However, NGOs, religious and secular alike, may make contributions to bridge-building and reconciliation at various levels that are of potentially greater importance than their role in delivering relief goods.

In the words of Norman E. Barth, Executive Director of Lutheran World Relief, reflecting on recent experience in the Sudan and Ethiopia, "The efforts of relief agencies are noble and necessary, but they are not enough. Such agencies must also become involved in the more difficult task of securing peace."

Chapter 6
The Sudan and Beyond

There may never be another Sudan, but there will need to be other Lifelines.

Lifeline is important in its own right as an energetic effort by the international community to provide humanitarian assistance in the Sudan's civil war. To what extent, however, does Lifeline's importance extend beyond the Sudan?

The Sudan is highly idiosyncratic, say some. There's no place like it on earth. A fortuitous but one-time convergence of circumstances made Lifeline possible in 1989. Within a few short months, the circumstances had changed to the point that Lifeline was barely sustainable even in the Sudan, much less replicable elsewhere.

Others claim that if the international community can put flesh on humanitarianism in the Sudan, it can do so anywhere. They believe that the state of siege there, while unlikely to recur elsewhere in precisely the same form, poses problems common to those faced by civilians and aid agencies in other civil wars.

In the view of the research team, Lifeline does indeed have broader significance. While capitalizing on a unique situation, Lifeline also embodied elements critical to the success of humanitarian interventions elsewhere. There may never be another Sudan, but there will need to be other Lifelines.

Looking to the wider horizon, then, it is useful to distill certain lessons from Lifeline for the nineties and beyond. The conclusions stated here rather briefly are the subject of a more detailed and technical report prepared under separate cover for the aid agencies.

First, the humanitarian principle of Lifeline, perhaps its major contribution, is enduring. Emerging in the nineteenth century and evolving since then in the cauldron of modern wars, it has

---

A Look to the Future

It is just as important today as it was last year at this time to make the world community aware of the great human tragedy in southern Sudan and to make every effort to have Sudan placed high on the agenda of world political concern. International pressure must be maintained and intensified before this conflict gets completely out of control and beyond resolution.

I fear that the Sudanese are not able to resolve this fratricidal conflict on their own, having not done so in over thirty years. Therefore it is imperative that the Sudan become the focus of a concerted international effort aimed at pressuring both sides to return to the peace table and begin the arduous task of building a just and lasting peace.

The chances of success may not be great, but the price for continued inattention by the world community will be massive human suffering without foreseeable end. We would then be forced to mount massive emergency relief operations ad infinitum to provide minimal survival to millions of victims of this costly civil conflict.

It would seem more productive to pressure both sides to pursue peace and national reconciliation which would create the secure environment needed for the nation to embark on the road to development and self-sufficiency. Only then will the need for emergency relief operations begin to diminish.

Internal NGO report from Khartoum, February 1990

been given fresh urgency and concreteness in the Sudan. Lifeline dramatizes the life-and-death importance of the right of civilians to receive humanitarian assistance and the right of impartial aid agencies to have access to them.

Those committed to protecting and extending this principle should anticipate certain challenges. The Lifeline experience suggests that humanitarian action can never be divorced from politics, which may both constrain and enhance responses to human need. Whatever the setting, political factors need to be more fully understood and more creatively harnessed to serve humanitarian interests. Rather than denying political realities, those committed to humanitarian values need to work to make the concern for human welfare a more potent political force in its own right.

Even in an era in which arbitrary actions by political authorities are drawing increasing fire, sovereignty is still likely to be invoked to parry efforts to put flesh on humanitarian principles. Protagonists in armed conflicts should be encouraged to use the sovereign rights they assert in order to facilitate relief activities. At the same time, all governments have humanitarian responsibilities that need to be more effectively met.

A commitment to humanitarian principle has implications for aid agencies ranging well beyond the programs they themselves administer. Preoccupation with humanitarian assistance operations to the exclusion of broader-gauge concerns for peace, human rights, and development will always be seductive. The root causes of suffering require a more conscientious and creative balance between providing aid and building on its potential for addressing much broader concerns.

Second, if humanitarian principle is not to be muddled in everyday practice, special skills are required of aid practitioners.

• A spirit of collaboration is necessary among humanitarian organizations that encourages and respects the distinctive contributions of each. From such collegiality should also flow a clearer division of labor among the various organizations of the UN system, governments, NGOs, and the ICRC and a greater appreciation for the comparative advantages of each. While the particular aid personnel thrust together in a given humanitarian emergency may be meeting for the first time, their institutions should not need to discover each other afresh with each new crisis.

• Higher levels of professionalism are required in all quarters. Lifeline suffered from a lack of such professionalism among some of those associated with it. A firmer commitment to humanitarian principle should help resist the temptation, even under duress, to resort to humanitarian petulance.

• Courageous leadership is needed by those committed to seeing that institutions respond more effectively to human needs. The demonstrated impact of dedicated and resourceful individuals, whether within governments or insurgent groups, NGOs or UN agencies, the media or the concerned public, provides encouragement to those who might otherwise distrust their own humanitarian instincts and equivocate on their own moral values.

At the same time, analysis of the Lifeline experience discloses structural problems and underlying tensions that, however carefully addressed, will probably never be fully overcome. Fundamental differences in approach to mission and mandate, constituencies and accountabilities, the legal and the moral will continue to make it impossible to mold all institutions into a single homogeneous unit. While greater understanding of such differences is essential, a variety of distinct channels needs to continue to be available for responding to crisis situations.

Third, Lifeline suggests that major humanitarian interventions into the fabric of societies, however necessary, can be expected to have mixed results. These need to be anticipated and hedged.

- Timing is critical. Governments deserve credit for seizing the moment with Lifeline but criticism for waiting so long. Moreover, even though Lifeline's late start-up required action at forced-pace cadence, operational decisions still should be framed in broader context.

- Transparency of action is essential, even though humanitarianism is difficult to divorce from other agendas and even though such action, however transparent, is not immune from criticism.

- Scale is crucial. International resource mobilization should not overwhelm indigenous capacity. Humanitarian theater on the world stage needs to support in-country responses appropriate to local needs, sensitivities, and constraints.

- Outsiders do not have a monopoly on concern for suffering. International presence and resources that provide protection and assistance should not preempt local capacity and responsibility. The tension between mounting emergency action and nurturing indigenous capacity cannot be routinely resolved in favor of the former.

- The most important contributions of a relief program may be the least quantifiable. Financial cost, narrowly calculated, can be a misleading indicator of ultimate value.

Fourth, Lifeline illuminates both the strengths and weaknesses of the existing system of international cooperation. Lifeline represented a tremendous investment of resources and energy in a single country-specific challenge. Contrasted with lesser attention to critical humanitarian needs in other countries, however, the response appears disproportionate.

The conclusion is not that the Sudan's civilians should have received no more attention than was accorded those caught in civil wars or natural disasters elsewhere. The message is rather that human life is precious and needs to be protected wherever endangered and from whatever quarter. The likelihood of continuing civil strife, with inordinate human and economic, social and political costs, will require a system that produces more balanced and well-proportioned responses by the international community to civilian populations in need wherever they are located.

Multilateral institutions are especially well situated for mobilizing action, for ensuring the protection of international law and the recognition of international humanitarian rights, and for mediating conflicts. The mandate of the UN system and its agencies in providing assistance, protection, and good offices in armed conflict settings needs to be strengthened and broadened.

The UN needs clearer authority to respond to human need without being seen to convey political recognition in doing so. Its agencies require fuller isolation from the bilateral agendas of governments, developed and developing, who for their own reasons wish to keep the UN on a short tether. However, the assumption that in settings of armed conflict the UN should automatically be given a coordinating mandate deserves review.

Lifeline also underscores the need for the UN to reflect more fully the diverse world in which it exists. The issue is not one of political theory but of pragmatic results. In responding to conflicts in which religious, cultural, ethnic, and political values are at issue, the institutions in the forefront need to be thoroughly universal in approach.

The Sudan experience reinforces the view that humanitarian concern is the common property of the international community, not the exclusive preserve of any one religious or cultural tradition or of economically more advanced societies. Humanitarian action that draws on the moral and cultural heritage of non-Western traditions is likely to prove more effective in advancing the values the West itself champions.

Fifth, ordinary people have an indispensable role in humanitarian action. The most essential initiatives are those which are taken by the people themselves. Their coping skills offer more hope for survival than the wizardry of relief specialists. While there are situations requiring outside assistance -- and the Sudan was without doubt one of them -- indigenous capacities are best enhanced by working to assure an environment free of violence and intimidation in which those capabilities can be exer-

A young boy who had sought shelter in April 1989 in the town of Wau.
ICRC/T. Gassmann

cised to the fullest. Local people themselves are ultimately the real lifeline.

Ordinary people outside the immediate crisis also have a pivotal role to play. The concerned public can be helpful both by pressing for action and by insisting on accountability. Within and outside the Sudan, they played an indispensable role in spurring action.

People are the final custodian of their common future, of the sovereignty of governments, and of what is done in their name. The ultimate test of humanitarian action is not what was intended by humanitarians but whether the results are judged positive by the beneficiaries themselves and sustained by them. People are the best safeguard for keeping the "human" in humanitarian.

Aid personnel associated with relief activities in the southern Sudan caution against making too much of Lifeline. UN officials themselves emphasize that the initiative was, after all, a set of specific programs hurriedly improvised to respond to the desperate needs of a particular besieged population.

Yet Lifeline was also a modern humanitarian milestone. As the world enters a decade during which divisions within nations are likely to upstage military conflicts between or among them, humanitarian assistance needs to gain wider acceptance as a legitimate and necessary activity.

In that context, Lifeline represents an important stage in the evolution of international humanitarian ethics and of practical strategies for safeguarding the rights of civilians besieged in situations of civil wars.

Appendix A
Key Dates
In Operation Lifeline Sudan

1989

March 8-9   Agreement on Operation Lifeline Sudan reached at Khartoum Conference by Sudan government, UN, and donor governments; costs of initiative projected at $55 million beyond the $78 million already in hand.

March 10   SPLM concurs in Lifeline at a separate meeting with UN officials in Addis Ababa, Ethiopia.

March 23   Appointment of James P. Grant as Personal Representative of the UN Secretary-General for Lifeline announced; donors meet at pledging conference in New York.

April 1   Lifeline officially launched with departure of truck convoy south from Khartoum; two days later a convoy heads north from Nairobi to the southern Sudan.

May 1   A cease fire, unilaterally declared by the SPLA, takes effect and lasts for six weeks.

May 28   Relief train with 1440 tons of food reaches Aweil after harrowing 9-day trip from Muglad.

June 1	Additional needs of $48 million confirmed, due in large part to unexpectedly high transport costs.
June 30	Prime Minister Sadiq el Mahdi overthrown by military coup.
July 2	Lieutenant-General Omar al-Bashir reaffirms new regime's commitment to Lifeline; declares unilateral truce for one month, later extended twice for periods of one month each.
July 11	Pledging conference in New York seeks additional funds for second half of year.
August 18	First barge convoy with relief supplies arrives at destination in Malakal.
August 21	Donor governments meet in New York to review Lifeline activities; similar meetings held earlier, April 11, May 2, June 13, and July 11.
September 27	UN Secretary-General submits report on Lifeline to UN General Assembly.
October 1	Grant turns over Lifeline duties to the Secretary-General's newly appointed Special Representative to the Sudan, Michael J. Priestley.
October 25	At request of the Sudan government, UN General Assembly unanimously agrees on continuation of Lifeline.
Late October	Lifeline reaches target of moving 107,000 tons of food to the southern Sudan; active hostilities resume.

November 2   Government closes Sudan airspace to relief flights pending review of "abuses" by Lifeline; other transport through corridors of tranquility also affected; soon thereafter, proposed international conference to extend Lifeline postponed indefinitely.

December   Government charges Lifeline with having smuggled arms to SPLA; UN and associated agencies deny charge. Contributions to Lifeline total $205 million at year's end.

1990

January   Warfare intensifies, causing renewed civilian displacement; SPLA steps up pressure on Juba; expatriate relief workers evacuated from Juba and other conflict areas.

March 26   After months of negotiations, the UN, the Sudan government, and other governments reach agreement at Khartoum Consultation on Lifeline 2.

March 30   SPLM/A affirm Lifeline 2 principles but withhold approval of proposed division of relief between the two sides.

April-May   UN relief flights resume April 9, ICRC flights May 4; other elements of Lifeline 2 gradually become operational.

INTERPLAY OF POLITICAL, MILITARY, AND HUMANITARIAN AGENDAS 1983-89

	Government of Sudan		Humanitarian Concerns	Sudan People's Liberation Movement	
	Military	Political		Political	Military
1983		Nimeiri regime introduces *sharia* (penal code based on Muslim law) throughout Sudan.	Severe drought in northern Sudan; drought in south as well.		Southerners within Sudanese army mutiny, SPLA formed.
1984	Skirmishes with SPLA units.	Domestic political pressures build (strikes, demonstrations, civil disobedience).	International response to drought and displacement brings some 50 NGOs to the Sudan. Khartoum authorities set up Relief and Resettlement Commission.	Vision articulated of a New Sudan as a means of resolving the nation's political, economic, and social problems.	Occasional skirmishes stepped up to low-intensity warfare.
1985	Government-armed militias join anti-SPLA activities.	Nimeiri deposed by military, which installs one-year Transitional Military Council under Gen. Swar ad-Dahab.	Displacement of civilians by militia activity accelerates. Sudan Relief and Rehabilitation Commission set up by SPLM.	Cease-fire rejected.	Warfare continues.

1986	Army under increasing military pressure from SPLA.	TMC declares cease fire but steps up military activity. National Islamic Front formed. Sadiq el Mahdi takes power after elections in north and parts of the south. Koka Dam Agreement lays basis of peace settlement, though government demurs and SPLM insists on more equitable development for neglected areas.	UN establishes Emergency Office for the Sudan in Khartoum. Drought-related suffering in western Sudan controlled. NGO and UN efforts to assess need in south and negotiate safe passage for relief with warring parties; relief convoys attacked. Operation Rainbow launched but flounders; UN official expelled; CART set up in Juba for distribution of relief.	Participation in elections refused. Agreement forged at Koka Dam near Addis Ababa with northern political parties (except National Islamic Front and Democratic Union Party).	Significant battlefield successes.
1987	Series of garrison towns falls.		Drought peaks in southern Sudan, but war and militia activities lead to upswing in displacement, death, and starvation.	Accord reached with the Sudan's African political parties.	Pace of military activity quickens. Siege laid to most towns in south remaining in government hands.

	Government of Sudan		Humanitarian Concerns	Sudan People's Liberation Movement	
	Military	Political		Political	Military
1987 cont.			Tribal militias kidnap and massacre civilians; recurrence of slavery of blacks by Arabs reported.		
			Efforts to arrange relief to war victims continue; further attacks on relief operations.		
			Four NGOs expelled for assisting in the south.		
1988	All towns in south except extreme western Equatoria and western Bahr el Ghazal under siege.	National Islamic Front strengthens role in government.	NGOs, religious groups, and political parties press for action on humanitarian and peace issues; limited relief operations to Juba and SPLA-controlled areas under way.	Agreement in Addis with Democratic Union Party provides political footing for SPLM in the north (November).	Series of towns captured, east bank of Nile and south of Sobat Rivers under SPLA control.
	Military losses increase army pressure on government for political settlement.	Ambo Conference widens political support for accord with SPLM.	Famine deaths reach new highs in northern Bahr El Ghazal and transition zone as people flee to the north and Ethiopia.		Fighting extended to areas in north which have their own grievances against Khartoum authorities.
			Government appeals to UN for humanitarian assistance (June).		

1989				
Government losses to SPLA continue; army issues ultimatum to el Mahdi.	Accord between Democratic Union Party and SPLM leaves National Islamic Front major remaining supporter of el Mahdi government.	Floods in Khartoum area attract international attention to those displaced by the war in the south (August).		SPLA in need of breather to consolidate control over recently captured territory.
		UN and Sudan government missions verify widespread malnutrition and massive famine deaths; seek to mobilize emergency relief.		
	Arrears to International Monetary Fund top $1 billion, to foreign creditors $10 billion; western donor governments increase pressure on government policies.	UN Secretary-General launches appeal for $73 million in relief aid (October).		
		After nine months of negotiations, ICRC reaches agreement with warring parties allowing relief to civilians in limited areas on both sides of conflict (December).		
		Pace of relief activities quickens.		
		Lifeline agreed to in March by government at Khartoum Conference and by SPLM in Addis.		
		Operations begin (April).		

Appendix C
Persons Consulted

I. Sudan Political Authorities

SUDAN GOVERNMENT

Revolutionary Command Council Chairman
    General Omar Hasan Ahmad Al-Bashir

Brigadier Pio Yukwan Deng
    Member of Revolutionary Command Council
    for National Salvation and
    Supervisor General, Council for the South

Dr. Abdalla Ahmed Abdalla
    Ambassador to the United States
    Washington, DC

Dr. Abdul Hamid Latif, Ambassador to Kenya

Ibrahim Abu Ouf, Commissioner
    Sudan Relief and Rehabilitation Commission

Nick Roberts, Technical Advisor
    Sudan Relief and Rehabilitation Commission

SUDAN PEOPLE'S LIBERATION MOVEMENT

Ashewil M. Banggol, Agricultural Coordinator, SRRA,
    Torit

James Duku, SRRA Liaison Officer, Nairobi

Majok Akop Kuol, Field Coordinator for Logistics and
    Transport, SRRA

Commander Riak Macar, SPLA, Nairobi

Kuol Manyang, SPLA Commander, Torit

Achol Marial, Medical Coordinator, SRRA, Kapoeta

Pierre Ohure, General Secretary, SRRA, Kapoeta

II. UNITED NATIONS SYSTEM

UNITED NATIONS

Abdulrahim A. Farah, Under-Secretary-General for Special Political Questions, Regional Co-operation, Decolonization and Trusteeship

F.T. Liu, Former Assistant Secretary-General for Special Political Questions

OPERATION LIFELINE SUDAN

Hassmi Choka, Radio Operator, Lokichoggio Station, Kenya

Nils Enqvist, OLS/WFP Regional Logistics Coordinator, Nairobi

Julio Delgado Idarraga, Convoy Leader, Southern Sector

Carlton James, Information/Media Coordinator, Nairobi

Peter Jobber, OLS/WFP Director of Operations, Khartoum

Michelle John, Project Officer (Health), Nairobi

Marcel R. LeCours, OLS/WFP Logistics Monitor, Khartoum

Robert McCarthy, OLS/UNICEF, Camp Manager, Lokichoggio

Thomas McKnight, OLS/UNICEF Project Officer, Nairobi

Myint Maung, OLS/UNICEF Liaison Officer, Kapoeta

Ruth Oloo, OLS/UNICEF Project Officer, Torit

Vincent E. O'Reilly, Coordinator Southern Sector Operations, Nairobi and UNICEF Chief of Operations

Detlev Palm, OLS/UNICEF, Project Officer, Nairobi

Mohammed Parvez, OLS/UNICEF, Supply/Logistics Officer, Nairobi

Adrian Pintos, OLS/UNICEF, Kapoeta

Babu Hailie Selassie, OLS/UNICEF, Project Officer, Bor

Willem Smit, OLS/WFP Logistics Monitor, Khartoum

Alastair Smith-Villers, OLS/WFP Project Officer, Nairobi

Patta Smith-Villers, OLS/WFP Project Officer, Nairobi

Humphrey Were, OLS/UNICEF Project Officer, Torit

UNITED NATIONS DEVELOPMENT PROGRAMME

Robert H. Brandstetter, Senior UN Adviser in Juba

Jane Wilder Jacqz, Senior Advisor, Division for Non-Governmental Organizations, Bureau for Programme Policy and Evaluation

Randolph C. Kent, Chief, Emergency Unit, Khartoum

Basem Khader, Chief, Division for Country Programmes Bureau for Arab States and European Programmes

Joana Merlin-Scholtes
Area Officer, Division for Country Programmes Bureau for Arab States and European Programmes

Michael J. Priestley, Special Representative of the UN Secretary-General
Resident Coordinator of the UN, Khartoum
Resident Representative, UNDP, the Sudan

Peter Schumann, Senior Project Management Officer, Office of Project Services
Former Official, UNDP Emergency Unit, Khartoum

W. Bryan Wannop, Senior Adviser
Division for Audit and Management Review
Former UNDP Resident Representative in the Sudan

UNICEF

James P. Grant, Executive Director

Ulf Kristofferrson, Chief of Emergency Programs, New York

Charles LaMuniere, Director of Emergency Programs, New York

Marjorie Newman-Black, Historian/Editor, New York

Farid Rahman, Sudan Representative, Khartoum

WORLD FOOD PROGRAMME

Khalid Adly, Senior Relief Officer, Disaster Relief Service, Operations Department, Rome

Robert C. Chase, Assistant Executive Director Operations Department, Rome

Anis Haider, Chief, Mediterranean and Middle East Bureau, Operations Department

James C. Ingram, Executive Director

Per Iversen, Chief of Transportation Resources and Transport Division, Rome

Jean-Pierre Nastorg, Chief, Evaluation Service Evaluation and Policy Division, Rome

Charles D. Paolillo, Director Evaluation and Policy Division, Rome

Bislow W. Parajuli, Logistics Officer Resources and Transport Division

Joseph Scalise, Evaluation Officer, Evaluation Service, Rome

D. John Shaw, Economic Adviser, Evaluation and Policy Division

Maas Van den Top, Director, Resources and Transport Division, Rome

III. OTHER GOVERNMENTS

CANADA

Francois Arsenault, Director, International Humanitarian Assistance Programme, Multilateral Programmes, CIDA

Larry Bennett, Officer, International Humanitarian Assistance Division, CIDA

Jean-Pierre Bolduc, Country Program Director, Maghreb and Regional Programs, Francophone Africa Branch, CIDA

Richard Chappell, Desk Officer, Anglophone Africa Relations, Ministry of External Affairs

Debbie Davis, Chief of Media Relations, Public Affairs Branch, CIDA

Ute Gerbrandt, Horn of Africa Desk, Anglophone Africa Branch, CIDA

Frank Gillis, Senior Program Officer, International Humanitarian Assistance, CIDA

W.D. Rolston, Program Development, Food Aid Centre, Multilateral Programmes Branch, CIDA

DENMARK

Erik Fil, Ambassador to Kenya

Birgitte Thygesen, First Secretary, Royal Danish Embassy, Kenya

KENYA

Bethuel Kiplagat, Permanent Secretary, Ministry of Foreign Affairs

KUWAIT

Abdalla Al-Suraya
Ambassador of the State of Kuwait to the Sudan

NETHERLANDS

Martin Koper, Third Secretary
Hans Nieman, Second Secretary
  Royal Netherlands Embassy, Kenya

SWEDEN

Karl Lostelius, Development Cooperation Officer
  Swedish International Development Authority, Nairobi

UNITED KINGDOM

John Beaven, Ambassador to Sudan

David B. G. Bell, Programmes Officer for Sudan and Uganda, Overseas Development Administration, Nairobi

Hamish S.T.C. Daniel, Second Secretary
  British Embassy, Khartoum

UNITED STATES

Norman Anderson, Former US Ambassador to the Sudan

Elizabeth Bassan, Program Officer, AID, Khartoum

Jack Davison, Director, African Affairs
  Africa Bureau, Department of State

Hunter Farnam, Former Official, OFDA

William Garvelink, Assistant Director, OFDA

Michael Harvey, Sudan Specialist, OFDA

Joseph Gettier, Sudan Specialist, OFDA

Fritz Gilbert, Deputy Mission Director, Khartoum

Lowell Lynch, Regional Food for Peace Officer, AID, Nairobi

Dayton Maxwell, Deputy Director, OFDA

Andrew Natsios, Director, OFDA

Julia Taft, Former Director, OFDA

IV. INTERGOVERNMENTAL ORGANIZATIONS

EUROPEAN COMMUNITY

Heather Elkins, Administrative Officer, Nairobi

Robert Baldwin, Sudan Desk Officer
Emergency Aid Division, Brussels

Brian Kelly, Acting Head of Division
Emergency Aid, Brussels

Asger Pilegaard, Head of Division
Directorate-General VIII, Development
Commission of the European Communities,
Brussels

Gary Quince, Sudan Desk Officer
Horn of Africa Division, Brussels

Elisabeth Tison, Food Aid Division, Brussels

ORGANIZATION OF AFRICAN UNITY

M.T. Mapuranga, Assistant Secretary-General
in charge of Education, Science, Culture and
Social Affairs

V. NON-GOVERNMENTAL ORGANIZATIONS

AFRICA WATCH (London)

Alex De Waal, Consultant

ALL AFRICA CONFERENCE OF CHURCHES (Nairobi)

Jose Chipenda, General Secretary
Harold Miller, Consultant

AFRICA FAITH AND JUSTICE NETWORK (Nairobi)

Sister Fredericka Jacob, NDM

AFRICA MEDICAL AND RESEARCH FOUNDATION (Nairobi)

Jayne Mutonga, Coordinator, Disaster Response Unit
Dr. Philip Rees, Director of Clinical Services

ASSOCIATION OF CHRISTIAN RESOURCE ORGANIZATIONS SERVING SUDAN (ACROSS) (Nairobi)

Dan Kelly, Executive Director
Russ Noble, Project Officer
Clement L. Wai-Wai, Project Officer

BREAD FOR THE WORLD (Washington, DC)

Sharon Pauling, Policy Analyst

CANADIAN COUNCIL FOR INTERNATIONAL CO-OPERATION (Ottawa)

Tim Brodhead, Executive Director
Tim Draman, Manager, Development Policy
Ian Filewood, Development Policy Officer

CATHOLIC DIOCESE OF TORIT

Bishop Taban Paride

CATHOLIC FUND FOR OVERSEAS DEVELOPMENT (CAFOD) (London)

Michael Medley, Project Officer
Robert Rees, Africa Project Department

CATHOLIC RELIEF SERVICES

Nyambura Githangui, Assistant Country Representative, Kenya, Sudan, and Uganda, Nairobi
Robert T. Quinlan, Senior Director, Geneva
Peter Shiras, Representative, Kenya, Sudan and Uganda
Berhe Tewolde, Head, Emergency Response Department, Nairobi

CHURCH WORLD SERVICE (Nairobi)

Virginia Cook, Regional Representative for East Africa and the Indian Ocean
Caleb Kahuthia, Director, Ecumenical Support Program for Sudan, Nairobi

DEVELOPMENT GROUP FOR ALTERNATIVE POLICIES (Washington, DC)

Gayle Smith, Coordinator Africa Program

DUTCH INTERCHURCH AID (Utrecht)

Jacques Willemse, Head, Emergency & Refugees Department

GERMAN EMERGENCY DOCTORS (Nairobi)

Eva Grozinger
A.J. van der Perk

HUMAN RIGHTS WATCH

Holly J. Burkhalter, Washington Director

INTERAID (Nairobi)

Julia Stewart

INTERNATIONAL CATHOLIC MIGRATION COMMISSION (Geneva)

Eugene Birrer
Andre Van Chau

INTERNATIONAL COMMITTEE FOR THE RED CROSS

Dominique Buff, Head of Delegation, Nairobi
Pierre Gassman, Delegate General for Africa, Nairobi
Harald Schmid de Gruneck, Deputy Delegate General for Africa, Geneva
Fred Isler, Deputy Head of Delegation, International Organizations, New York
Andreas Lendorff, Head of Relief Division, Geneva
Vincent Nicod, Delegate, Geneva

INTERNATIONAL COUNCIL OF VOLUNTARY AGENCIES (Geneva)

Tony Kozlowski, Executive Director
Jean-Pierre de Warlincourt, Senior Program Associate

INTERNATIONAL RESCUE COMMITTEE (Nairobi)

Colette Byrne, Medical Director
Scott Portman, Program Director
Ann Zimmerman, Accountant/Health Trainer

ISLAMIC AFRICAN RELIEF AGENCY (Khartoum)

Abdalla Suliman El Awad, Director General
Gazuli D'Faallah, Chairman of Board of Directors
Former Prime Minister of the Sudan
Ali Tamin Fartak, Board Member. Former Government Official and Member, National Peace Dialogue and National Islamic Front

LEAGUE OF RED CROSS AND RED CRESCENT SOCIETIES

John Lloyd, 3rd, Geneva
Bruce Miller, Head of Delegation, Khartoum
Ibrahim Osman, Head of Africa Department, Geneva

LICROSS/VOLAGS STEERING COMMITTEE FOR DISASTERS (Geneva)

Robert J.B. Rossborough, Consultant and Secretary

LUTHERAN WORLD FEDERATION

Johan Balslev, Secretary for Emergency Projects,
    Geneva
Robert G. Koepp, Director of Sudan Emergency
    Operations, Nairobi
Kaanaeli Makundi, Geneva
Admasu Simeso, Geneva

LUTHERAN WORLD RELIEF

Sigurd Hansen, Regional Representative, Nairobi
Norman E. Barth, Executive Director, New York

MARYKNOLL FATHERS & BROTHERS (Nairobi)

Carroll Houle, Africa Area Coordinator

MEDIC (Comité Internationale Medicale pour l'Urgence et Developpement)

Bruce Pike, Torit

MÉDICINS SANS FRONTIÈRES-HOLLAND (Nairobi)

Johan Hesselink, Program Coordinator
Kees Posthuma, Medical Coordinator

MÉDICINS SANS FRONTIÈRES-FRANCE (Nairobi)

Jean-Christophe Adrian, Represenative

MENNONITE CENTRAL COMMITTEE (Nairobi)

William Reimer, Sudan Country Representative

MISSIONARY AVIATION FELLOWSHIP (Nairobi)

Doug Wakeling

NATIONAL COUNCIL OF CHURCHES OF KENYA (Nairobi)

Samuel Kobia, General Secretary

NORWEGIAN CHURCH AID (Nairobi)

Svein Tore Rode-Christoffersen, Manager
George Waweru, Logistics Officer

NORWEGIAN PEOPLE'S AID (Nairobi)

Sharif Egal, Logistics Officer
Egil Hagen, Resident Representative, Nairobi
Abdi Hassan, Transporter

OXFAM-UK

David De Pury, Country Representative, Khartoum
Richard Graham, Relief Coordinator, Khartoum
Jane Green, Former Emergency Liaison Officer, Nairobi
Anthony Nedley, Regional Representative, Southern Sudan
Margaret Mudogo, Emergency Liaison Officer, Nairobi

REFUGEE POLICY GROUP

Jacques Cuenod, Geneva
Susan Forbes-Martin, Washington, DC
Dennis Gallagher, Executive Director, Washington, DC

SAVE THE CHILDREN (UK)

Ben Foote, Regional Representative, Nairobi

SUDANAID (Khartoum)

Asma Dallalah, Executive Director

SUDANESE RED CRESCENT SOCIETY (Khartoum)

Ahmed Adam Gizo, Acting Secretary General

SUDAN COUNCIL OF CHURCHES (Khartoum)

Ezekiel Kutjok, General Secretary

US COMMITTEE FOR REFUGEES (Washington)

Roger Winter, Director

WORLD ALLIANCE OF YMCAs (Geneva)

Frank Kiehne
Joel Kinagwi

WORLD COUNCIL OF CHURCHES (Geneva)

Nico Keulemans, Emergencies Officer, Commission on
Interchurch Aid, Refugees, and World Service
(CICARWS)
Melaku Kifle, Africa Secretary, CICARWS
Abel Mbilinyi, African Refugees Secretary, CICARWS

WORLD VISION INTERNATIONAL

Leo Ballard, Associate Director, Relief Operations East
Africa, Nairobi
Russell Kerr, Director/Relief, Monrovia, California
H. Dwight Swartzendruber, Regional Senior Advisor,
Maputo, Mozambique

VI. MEDIA

Africa Confidential (London)

Gillian Lusk, Deputy Editor

The Nation (Nairobi)

John Gachie, Foreign Editor

Kenya Times (Nairobi)

Philip Ochieng, Editor-in-Chief
Edmund Kwena, Foreign Editor
Charles Kulundu, Former Foreign Editor

The Sudan Times (Khartoum, now banned)

Bona Malwal, Editor

Voice of America (Nairobi)

Jim Malone, Correspondent and
Former Chairman, Foreign Correspondents'
Association

Financial Times (Nairobi)

Julian Ozanne

New York Times (Nairobi)

Jane Perlez

British Broadcasting Corporation

Lucy Hannan, Nairobi

VII. OTHERS

Representative Gary Ackerman, US House of Representatives, Washington, DC

Joseph Beraki, relief worker, Nairobi

Frederick C. Cuny, International Technical Consultants for Emergency Management, Dallas, Texas

Francis M. Deng, Senior Fellow, the Brookings Institution, Washington and Former Sudan Minister of State for Foreign Affairs

Barbara Hendrie, private consultant, London

David Melvill, Relief and Development Services International, Inc., Orleans, Canada

Michael Myers, Counsel, Immigration and Refugee Subcommittee, Senate Judiciary Committee, Washington

The above listing is a partial one, since some individuals interviewed requested that their names and organizations not be referenced in this study.

Appendix D
Contributing Agencies

The following agencies have supported the Operation Lifeline
Sudan Case Study with cash and/or in-kind contributions:

Church World Service
The Institute for International Studies, Brown University
The International Council of Voluntary Agencies
The Lutheran World Federation
Lutheran World Relief
The Mennonite Central Committee
The Netherlands International Development Agency
The Refugee Policy Group
Sudan working group/Canadian Council for International
    Co-operation
The Swedish International Development Authority
The United Nations Children's Fund
The United Nations Development Programme
The United Nations World Food Programme

Appendix E
Resources for Further Reference

Africa Watch. *Sudan: A Human Rights Disaster*. New York and Washington: The Africa Watch Committee, 1990.

Adams, Barbara, and Lent, Marina. *Accounting for Africa at the United Nations: A Guide for NGOs*. American Friends Service Committee: Philadelphia, 1988.

Ahmed, Abel Ghaffar and Sorbo, Gunnar M. (eds.) *Management of the Crisis in the Sudan*. Bergen, Norway: University of Bergen, 1989.

Al-Rahim, Muddathir Abd; Badel, R.; Mardall, Adlan; and Woodward, P. *Sudan since Independence*. Aldershot: Gower, 1986.

Allen, Tim. *War and Peace in Southern Sudan*. Kampala, Uganda: Makerere Institute of Social Research, 1987.

Amnesty International. *Sudan: Human Rights Violations in the Context of Civil War*. New York: Amnesty International, 1989.

Anderson, Mary B., and Woodrow, Peter J. *Rising from the Ashes: Development Strategies in Times of Disaster*. Boulder, CO and San Francisco, CA: Westview, 1989.

Beshir, Mohamed Omer. *The Southern Sudan: Background to Conflict*. London: C. Hurst & Co.; Khartoum: Al-Ayam Press, 1968.

-----. *The Southern Sudan: From Conflict to Peace.* Khartoum: The Khartoum Bookshop, 1975.

-----. *The Southern Sudan, regionalism, and religion.* London: University of Khartoum Graduate College, 1984. [Distributed by Ithaca Press]

Beshir, Mohamed Omer, ed. "Sudan, aid and external relations: selected essays." Monograph No. 9, University of Khartoum Graduate College, London: distributed by Ithaca Press, 1984.

Bonner, Raymond. "Famine." *The New Yorker*, March 13, 1989.

Bratton, Michael. "Politics of Government/NGO Relations in Africa," *World Development*, April 1989 (Vol. 17: No 4).

Cater, Nick: *Sudan, the roots of famine.* Oxford: Oxfam, 1986.

Collins, R.O. *Shadows in the Grass: Britain in the Southern Sudan, 1918-1956.* New Haven: Yale University Press, 1983.

Daly, M.W. *Modernization in the Sudan.* New York: Lilian Barber Press, 1985.

De Waal, Alexander. *Famine That Kills: Darfur, Sudan 1984-85.* Oxford: Clarendon Press, 1989.

Deng, Francis Malwal. *The Man Called Deng Majok: A Biography of Power, Polygamy, and Change.* New Haven, CT: Yale University Press, 1986.

----. *Seeds of Redemption.* New York: Lilian Barber Press, 1986.

Fraser, Colin. *Lifelines... For Africa Still in Peril and Distress.* London: Hutchinson, 1988.

Garang, John. *John Garang Speaks*. London, New York: KPI, 1987.

Gill, Peter. *A Year in the Death of Africa*. London: Paladin/Grafton Books, 1986.

Giorgis, Dawit Wolde. *Red Tears: War, Famine and Revolution in Ethiopia*. Trenton, NJ: Red Sea Press, 1988.

Hendrie, Barbara. "Cross-border Relief Operations in Eritrea and Tigray," in *Disasters*, (Vol. 13, No. 4, 1989).

Holt, P.M. and Daly, M.W. *A History of the Sudan*. London, New York: Longman, 1988 (Fourth edition).

Horn of Africa Project. *'Facing' the Enemy: Conflict Resolution Rooted in the Horn of Africa*. Waterloo, Ontario, Canada: Institute of Peace and Conflict Studies, Conrad Grebel College, 1989.

Independent Commission on International Humanitarian Issues. *Famine: A Man-made Disaster*. London and Atlantic Highlands, NJ: Zed Books, 1985. [The Commission's address is P.O. Box 83, 1211 Geneva 20, Switzerland.]

----. *Modern Wars: The Humanitarian Challenge*. London and Atlantic Highlands, NJ: Zed Books, 1988.

----. *Winning the Human Race?* London and Atlantic Highlands, NJ: Zed Books, 1986.

Jansson, Kurt; Harris, Michael; and Penrose, Angela. *The Ethiopian Famine*. London and Atlantic Highlands, NJ: Zed Books, 1987.

Johnson, Douglas H. "The Future of the Southern Sudan's Past," *Africa Today*, Vol. 28, No. 2, 1981.

Kalshoven, Frits, ed. *Assisting the Victims of Armed Conflict and Other Disasters.* Dordrecht, Netherlands, Boston, and London: Martinus Nijhoff Publishers, 1989.

Kaplan, Robert D. *The Wars behind the Famine.* Boulder, CO: Westview Press, 1988.

Kent, Randolph C. *Anatomy of Disaster.* London, New York: Pinter Publishers, 1987.

Khalid, Mansour. *Nimeiri and the Revolution of May.* London: KPI, 1985.

Life and Peace Institue. "The Search for Peace in the Horn of Africa." Uppsala, Sweden: *Life and Peace Review*, Vol. 2, No. 3, 1988 [Box 297, S-751 05, Uppsala].

Lavergne, Marc, ed. *Le Soudan Contemporain.* Paris: Karthala, 1989.

Lusk, Gill. "The Sudan War: Death in the South." London: Catholic Fund for Overseas Development (CAFOD), 1987.

Mahmud, Ushari Ahmed, and Baldo, Suleyman Ali. *Al Daien Massacre: Slavery in the Sudan.* Khartoum: privately printed, 1987.

Malwal, Bona. *People and Power in Sudan: The Struggle for National Stability.* London: Ithaca Press, 1981.

----. *The Sudan: A Second Challenge to Nationhood.* New York: Thornton Books, 1985.

Markakis, John. "Famine and Politics in the Horn of Africa," in *Capital and Class*, No. 31, Spring, 1987, pp. 16-23.

Minear, Larry. *Helping People in an Age of Conflict: Toward a New Professionalism in US Voluntary Humanitarian Assistance.* InterAction: New York and Washington, 1988.

Minority Rights Group. "The Southern Sudan." Report No. 78. London, 1988. [379 Brixton Road, London SW9 7DE, UK]

Niblock, Thomas. *Class and Power in Sudan: The Dynamics of Sudanese Politics, 1898-1985.* London: MacMillan, 1987.

Peace in Sudan Group. *War in Sudan: An analysis of conflict. London: Peace in Sudan Group, 1990.* [The group's address is BM Peace in Sudan, London WC1N 3XX]

Saud, Joseph, and Pillsbury, Barbara L.K., eds. *Muslim-Christian Conflicts.* Kent, England: Dawson, 1978.

Sudan Democratic Gazette: A Newsletter for Democratic Pluralism. [P.O. Box 2295, London W14 0ND, UK.]

Timberlake, Lloyd. *Africa in Crisis: The Causes, the Cures of Environmental Bankruptcy.* London and Washington: Earthscan, 1985.

Twose, Nigel and Pogrund, Benjamin. *War Wounds: Development Costs of Conflict in Southern Sudan.* London, Paris, and Washington: Panos Institute, 1988.

Woodward, Peter, ed. *Sudan Since Nimeiri.* London: Croom Helm, 1990.

Woodward, Peter. *Sudan, 1898-1989: The Unstable State.* London: L. Crook Academic Pub., 1990.

Appendix F
Members of the Operation Lifeline Sudan Case Study Team

Tabyiegen Agnes Abuom (Kenya) is a senior research fellow of the University of Uppsala, Sweden. Her training includes college and post-graduate degrees from Uppsala, with advanced work in development economics and history. Currently based in Nairobi, her work experience has involved assignments with the World Council of Churches, the Sudan Council of Churches, and the Swedish International Development Authority. She has served as a research fellow at the University of Zimbabwe in Harare and is currently a facilitator for East Africa in the Southern Networks for Development.

Eshetu Chole (Ethiopia) teaches in the Department of Economics at Addis Ababa University. Following undergraduate work there, he received advanced economics degrees from the University of Illinois and Syracuse. He is active in numerous professional associations and serves as executive secretary of the Organization for Social Science Research in East Africa and as editor of the *Eastern Africa Social Science Research Review*. He has written extensively on issues of economics and development in Ethiopia and Africa and has served as a consultant to UN agencies, non-governmental groups, and research institutions.

Kosti Manibe (Sudan) is currently on leave from duties as Deputy General Secretary of the Sudan Council of Churches, based in Khartoum. He has worked with the Council in a variety of capacities since 1978. He is a graduate in the arts from Makerere University in Kampala and has a diploma from the Khartoum School of Mass Communication. Following employment with the Sudan Government's Ministry of Information and Culture in Khartoum, he served for three years as editor of the *Nile Mirror* newspaper. He contributed a chapter on "The Agony of the Family" to *War Wounds*, listed in the bibliography.

Larry Minear (US) is representative for development policy of Church World Service and Lutheran World Relief, based in Washington, DC. Trained in literature, history, and ethics at Yale and Harvard Universities, he assisted in post-civil war resettlement activities in the Sudan in 1972-73. He has served as a consultant to various UN agencies and US government task forces. During the years 1985-87 he assisted US private aid groups in reviewing problems of providing humanitarian assistance in situations of armed conflict. He has written extensively on humanitarian and development issues and served as team leader for the Case Study.

Abdul Mohammed (Ethiopia) is a peace activist based in Nairobi. With undergraduate and graduate economics degrees from Queens College and the New School for Social Research of New York, he has worked in refugee resettlement for Church World Service and served as director of relief and emergencies for the Sudan Council of Churches (1985-89). He has been a consultant on emergency programs, refugees, capacity-building, and food security to UNICEF, WFP, and UNDP and to non-governmental groups and the Ford Foundation. He is currently establishing the Inter-Africa Group to promote humanitarian assistance, development, and peace in the Horn of Africa. The originator of the idea of the Operation Lifeline Sudan Case Study, he played the lead role in assembling the research team.

Jennefer Sebstad (US) is a Nairobi-based independent consultant working with non-governmental groups on enterprise development and women's programs. Her academic training includes undergraduate studies in geography at the University of Michigan and graduate work in urban and regional planning at the University of California, Los Angeles. Her work experience includes assignments with the Ford Foundation, the US Agency for International Development, the World Bank, the International Center for Research on Women (Washington, DC), and the Self Employed Women's Association (Ahmedabad, India).

Thomas G. Weiss (US) is Associate Director of the Institute for International Studies at Brown University in Providence, Rhode Island. With undergraduate work in economics and advanced degrees in public affairs, he has served with the UN Conference on Trade and Development, the UN Commissioner for Namibia, the UN Institute for Training and Research, and the International Labor Organization. For a number of years he was the executive director of the International Peace Academy in New York City. He has taught and written extensively in the fields of international conflict management, negotiations, development, peace-keeping, organization, and political economy.

Serving in their personal capacities, members of the team participated in the Case Study between March 15 and June 30, 1990. Based in Nairobi, the team conducted interviews as well in the Sudan, Addis Ababa, Rome, Geneva, Brussels, London, New York, Washington, and Ottawa. Under separate cover, the team is providing a more detailed set of recommendations for aid agencies.

Glossary

ACROSS	Association of Christian Resource Organizations Serving Sudan
AID	US Agency for International Development
AMI	Assistance Medicale Internationale
CAFOD	The Catholic Fund for Overseas Development
CART	Combined Agencies Relief Team
CIDA	Canadian International Development Agency
EC	European Community
FAO	United Nations Food and Agriculture Organization
IARA	Islamic African Relief Agency
ICRC	International Committee of the Red Cross
IMF	International Monetary Fund
LICROSS	League of Red Cross and Red Crescent Societies
LWF	Lutheran World Federation
MSF	Médicins sans Frontières
NIF	National Islamic Front
NGO	Non-Governmental Organization
NPA	Norwegian People's Aid
OAU	Organization of African Unity
OFDA	US Office of Foreign Disaster Assistance
OLS	Operation Lifeline Sudan
RRC	The Sudan Government's Relief and Resettlement Commission
SCC	The Sudan Council of Churches
SCOVA	The Sudan Council of Voluntary Agencies
SPLA	The Sudan People's Liberation Army
SPLM	The Sudan People's Liberation Movement
SPLM/A	The Sudan People's Liberation Movement/Army
SRRA	The Sudan Relief and Rehabilitation Association of the SPLM
UK	United Kingdom

UN	United Nations
UNDP	United Nations Development Programme
UNHCR	United Nations High Commissioner for Refugees
UNDRO	United Nations Disaster Relief Organization
UNICEF	United Nations Children's Fund
US	United States
USSR	Union of Soviet Socialist Republics
WFP	United Nations World Food Programme

Footnotes

1. For further background, see Peace in Sudan Group, *War in Sudan: An Analysis of the Conflict* (London, 1990) and other resources listed in Appendix E.

2. *New African*, October 1989, p. 13.

3. For further details, see Africa Watch, *Sudan: A Human Rights Disaster* (New York and Washington, 1990), pp. 101-137.

4. Cf. Economist Intelligence Unit, Sudan: Country Profile 1990-91, *Annual Survey*, and UN Development Program, *Human Development Report 1990* (New York and Oxford: Oxford University Press, 1990).

5. Excerpted and adapted from Conradin Perner, "Journal," Lokichoggio/Nairobi, March 20, 1989 (ICRC: Geneva, unprinted) pp. 5, 9, 10.

6. Executive Secretary Adebayo Adedeji of the UN Economic Commission for Africa, as quoted in Ernest Harsch, "African Economy Still Struggling Uphill," in *Africa Recovery* (vol. 3, no. 3, December 1989), pp. 1, 19.

7. World Bank, *World Development Report* (New York and Oxford: Oxford University Press, 1989), pp. 12-3.

8. US Committee for Refugees, *World Refugee Survey: 1989 in Review* (Washington, USCR, 1990), p. 31.

Chapter 2

1. W. Bryan Wannop, "Report on the First Muglad-Aweil Train," UN Development Programme, June 29, 1989, p. 5.

2. Thorvald Stoltenberg, "In Search of Security," *Refugees*, March 1990, p. 9.

3. International Institute for Environment and Development, *Report on the African Emergency Relief Operation 1984-1986* (London and Washington, IIED, 1986), p. 7.

Chapter 3

1. Independent Commission on International Humanitarian Issues, *Winning the Human Race?* (London and Atlantic Highlands, NJ, Zed Books, 1988), p. 11. [This and later citations used by permission of the Independent Commission.]

2. Gill Lusk, "The War Grinds On," *Middle East International*, March 30, 1990, p. 14.

3. Raymond Bonner, "Famine," *The New Yorker*, March 13, 1989, p. 87.

4. Salim Salim, Address to the 51st Session of the OAU Council of Ministers, February 1990, in "Stop the Suffering!", *Refugees*, May 1990, p. 8.

5. Pieter Bukman, in Frits Kalshoven, ed., *Assisting the Victims of Armed Conflict and Other Disasters* (Dordrecht, Boston, London, Martinus Nijhoff, 1989), p. 7. [This and later citations reprinted by permission of Kluwer Academic Publishers.]

6. Marcus Thompson, "Cooperation and Coordination: Oxfam's Views," in Kalshoven, ed., op.cit., p. 178.

7. Peter Macalister-Smith, "Rights and Duties of the Agencies Involved in Providing Humanitarian Assistance and their Personnel in Armed Conflict," in Kalshoven, ed., op.cit., p. 104.

8. Resolution, Canadian Council for International Co-operation, May 10, 1990, p. 1.

Chapter 4

1. Raymond Bonner, op.cit., p. 86.

2. Operation Lifeline Sudan, Situation Report No. 8, p. 7 (Nairobi: undated).

3. Independent Commission, op.cit., pp. 71-72.

4. Report of the Secretary-General, "Emergency Assistance to the Sudan: Operation Lifeline Sudan," General Assembly Document A/44/571, Sept. 27, 1989, pp. 13-14.

5. Marcus Thompson, op.cit., p. 177.

6. Reginald Moreels, "Humanitarian Diplomacy: The Essence of Humanitarian Assistance," in Kalshoven, ed., op.cit., pp. 46-7.

7. Bernard Kouchner, "Morals of Urgent Need," in Kalshoven, ed., op.cit., p. 55.

8. Marcus Thompson, op.cit., p. 177.

9. Hendrie elaborates this point in "Cross-border Relief Operations in Eritrea and Tigray," in *Disasters*, (Vol. 13, No. 4, 1989).

10. Additional Protocol I (1977) to the Geneva Conventions (1949): "Victims of International Armed Conflicts," Article 70, Section 1; quoted in Kalshoven, ed., op.cit., p. 226.

11. Quoted in Paul J. I. M. de Waart, "Long-term Development Aspects of Humanitarian Assistance in Armed Conflicts," in Kalshoven, op. cit., p. 71.

12. Peter Macalister-Smith, op.cit., p. 100.

13. Independent Commission, op.cit., pp. 189-90.

14. Ibid., p. 9.

Chapter 5

1. Gill Lusk, "Operation Lifeline," *Middle East International*, April 14, 1989, p. 13.

2. Operation Lifeline Sudan, Situation Report No. 8, p. 7 (Nairobi, undated).

3. US Department of State, *Country Reports on Human Rights Practices for 1988* (Washington, DC, 1989), p. 345.

4. Amnesty International, *Sudan: Human Rights Violations in the Context of Civil War* (New York, 1989), p. 7.

5. Salim Salim, op.cit., p. 8.

6. Frits Kalshoven and Charlotte Siewertsz van Reesema, "Summary of Discussions," in Kalshoven, ed., op.cit., p. 204.

7. SPLM/SPLA Press Statement on Operation Lifeline Sudan, March 18, 1990, p. 1.

Index